Responding to Loss

A learning and development manual

2nd Edition

Bernard Moss
& Neil Thompson

Responding to Loss

A learning and development manual, 2nd edition

Published by:
Pavilion Publishing and Media Ltd
Blue Sky Offices
Cecil Pashley Way
Shoreham by Sea
West Sussex
BN43 5FF
UK

Tel: 01273 434 943
Fax: 01273 227 308

First published 2019

A catalogue record for this book is available from the British Library.

ISBN: 978-1-912755-44-8

Pavilion Publishing and Media is a leading publisher of books, training materials and digital content in mental health, social care and allied fields. Pavilion and its imprints offer must-have knowledge and innovative learning solutions underpinned by sound research and professional values.

Authors: Bernard Moss and Neil Thompson
Production editor: Mike Benge, Pavilion Publishing and Media Ltd.
Cover design: Emma Dawe, Pavilion Publishing and Media Ltd.
Page layout and typesetting: Emma Dawe, Pavilion Publishing and Media Ltd.
Printing: Ashford Press

Contents

List of resources

All the resources needed to run the exercises in this book can be found at www.pavpub.com/learning-from-practice-resources

Slides

Slide 1: Some basic ground rules

Slide 2: Great expectations

Slide 3: The Dual Process Approach

Slide 4: The idea of stages

Slide 5: The tasks of grief

Slide 6: Finding new meanings

Slide 7: Disenfranchised grief

Slide 8: Staff care

Slide 9: Returning to work – personal anxieties

Slide 10: Returning to work – Managers' and colleagues' anxieties

Slide 11: Dealing with the aftermath

Worksheets

Worksheet 1: Listing the losses

Worksheet 2: Codes of practice

Worksheet 3: Trying to make sense of it all

Worksheet 4: Out of the ordinary (1)

Worksheet 5: Out of the ordinary (2)

Worksheet 6: Where do I feature in all this?

Worksheet 7: Responding to loss

Worksheet 8: It's got nothing to do with us

Worksheet 9: The conspiracy of silence (1)

Worksheet 10: The conspiracy of silence (2)

Worksheet 11: Men are from Mars…

Worksheet 12: Leaving was hard… But coming back was even worse

Handouts

Handout 1: Approach 1: The Dual Process Model

Handout 2: Approach 2: The idea of stages

Handout 3: Approach 3: The tasks of grief

Handout 4: Approach 4: Finding new meaning

Handout 5: My boss really cares

Handout 6: Returning to work

Introduction

About the series

The *Learning from Practice* series offers a range of training and development resources for trainers, tutors and others involved in promoting learning. Each manual has been developed to serve as the basis for a training course, a staff development event and/or as part of a university or college module. Each of them assumes no specialist knowledge, either of the subject matter or of learning theory, although it is expected that users of the manual will have at least some familiarity with what is involved in running a training course or similar event.

Each manual contains useful background information about the subject matter covered so that the user of the resources can approach the subject matter with at least a basic knowledge of the key issues and, it is hoped, a desire to find out more from other available sources (which is why each manual has a Guide to further learning near the end, see p95). This background information is then followed by a series of exercises, each of which has step-by-step guidance for using the ideas in practice during an event.

There are also supplementary materials, although these will vary from manual to manual. Some have a PowerPoint file that can be used to form the basis of any presentations that need to be made as part of one or more exercises.

Of course, it is likely that experienced educators will want to consider adapting, extending, or even combining elements from the various exercises, and this can potentially work well. However, any such changes will need to be thought through very carefully and inexperienced trainers or tutors should perhaps run the exercises at least once as they stand before making any changes.

The series was originally published by Russell House Publishing, but this manual forms part of a set of new, revised and updated editions published by Pavilion Publishing and Media as part of their range of high-quality learning and development resources.

The first editions of these resources were very well received, with considerable positive feedback. We trust you will find this new edition equally helpful, if not more so, and we wish you well in using the materials

Other titles in the series

Developing Leadership by Peter Gilbert and Neil Thompson

Promoting Equality, Valuing Diversity by Neil Thompson

Reflective Supervision by Neil Thompson and Peter Gilbert

Spirituality, Meaning and Values by Bernard Moss and Neil Thompson

Tackling Bullying and Harassment in the Workplace by Neil Thompson

Working with Adults: Values into Practice by Sue Thompson and Jackie Robinson

About this manual

Loss and grief are inescapable parts of life, and yet so often they get swept under the carpet. So many people behave as if loss and grief are unfortunate accidents that occur in certain people's lives from time to time, rather than fundamental parts of everybody's life.

The impact of grief can be short term and clearly visible, as in the aftermath of a bereavement, for example. However, the effects of grief – especially grief arising from cumulative, multiple or traumatic losses – can still be felt years later and can be operating unnoticed because of the lack of any immediate connection with a specific loss. Members of the 'people professions' – that is, the helping professions plus managers, supervisors, leaders and human resource professionals across the various sectors – would therefore be well advised to take note of the significance of grief and how it affects individuals, families, groups and even organisations. This manual is an aid to doing just that.

Written by two authors who have rightly earned a reputation for writing clearly and helpfully about complex matters without oversimplifying them, this manual offers excellent guidance on how to put such matters on the agenda. With a wealth of experience of dealing with and teaching about the impact of loss on people's lives, the authors have been able to provide a very well-informed and user-friendly set of training and development resources.

This important publication should be of interest to two groups of trainers, tutors and teachers. First, there will be those supporting people whose working lives are expected to bring them into direct contact with loss issues (hospice workers, nurses, social workers, counsellors, teachers, youth workers, the emergency services and so on). The second group, however, is much broader, and consists of those working with anyone who is likely to encounter loss in their working lives at some point – and that means pretty much anyone!

This means managers and human resource professionals wanting to ensure the smooth and effective running of their organisations: any employee in any setting who wishes to support colleagues experiencing difficulties brought about by loss; specialist support staff such as occupational health professionals and occupational psychologists and counsellors; trade unionists wishing to support their members; and, of course, members of the helping professions who are likely to encounter the effects of grief on a fairly regular basis. This manual therefore offers guidance to all corners of the working world – as a guide for those organisations that are attuned to the significance of loss and grief in relation to both their own employees and the people they serve (clients, patients, service users, carers and so on) and as an aid to raising awareness for those organisations that have yet to learn just how significant a factor grief is within the workplace.

In other words, this is not so much a specialist resource for those who are directly involved in dealing with loss. It also offers invaluable guidance everyone, for no-one is immune to loss and grief, and the sooner organisations recognise this the better. I have been fortunate to work with someone of the calibre of Bernard Moss to develop the second edition of this manual, to help us deal with these complex and sensitive issues.

Dr Neil Thompson
Series editor

The series editor

Dr Neil Thompson is an independent writer, educator and adviser. He has previously held full or honorary professorships at four UK universities and is now a sought-after trainer, consultant and conference speaker.

He has qualifications in social work; training and development; mediation and alternative dispute resolution; and management (MBA); as well as a first-class honours degree, a doctorate (PhD) and a higher doctorate (DLitt). In 2011 he was presented with a Lifetime Achievement Award by BASW Cymru and in 2014 he was presented with the Dr Robert Fulton Award for excellence in the field of death, dying and bereavement from the Center for Death Education and Bioethics at the University of Wisconsin-La Crosse. He is a Fellow of the Chartered Institute of Personnel and Development and the Higher Education Academy and a Life Fellow of the Royal Society of Arts and the Institute of Welsh Affairs. In addition, he is a member of the International Work Group on Death, Dying and Bereavement.

Neil is a highly respected author, with over 300 publications to his name, including several bestselling books. His recent publications include *The Social Worker's Practice Manual* (Avenue Media Solutions, 2018), *Mental Health and Well-being: Alternatives to the medical model* (Routledge, 2019) and *The Learning from Practice Manual* (Avenue Media Solutions, 2019).

He has been a speaker at conferences and seminars in the UK, Ireland, Italy, Spain, Norway, the Netherlands, Greece, the Czech Republic, Turkey, India, Hong Kong, Canada, the United States and Australia.

In his current role Neil offers:

▶ training, consultancy, mediation and expert witness services

▶ E-learning courses.

▶ The Avenue Professional Development Programme – a subscription-based online learning community based on principles of self-directed learning and geared towards developing critically reflective practice

▶ online survey services to help organisations gauge how well they are doing in their people management efforts

▶ coaching and mentoring.

Information about his work, services and resources is available at: www.NeilThompson. info. He has a YouTube channel at https://bit.ly/2O0E6OR, and a free subscription to his humansolutions e-newsletter can be obtained at: www.humansolutions.org.uk.

The authors

Bernard Moss is Professor Emeritus of Social Work Education and Spirituality at Staffordshire University where he began working with social work students in 1993. His particular teaching interests have focused on communications skills, studies in death, dying and bereavement, and mediation studies. He was formerly the Director of the Centre for Spirituality and Health at Staffordshire University and made significant contributions to debates on this important theme. In 2004 he was awarded a National Teaching Fellowship by the Higher Education Academy to mark his teaching excellence and became a senior fellow in 2007.

Bernard's earlier career included being a probation officer, a relationship counsellor, a mediator and a leader of a faith community. His publications include *Communication Skills for Health and Social Care* (4th edn, Sage, 2017) and, with Neil Thompson, *Spirituality, Meaning and Values: A learning and development manual* (2nd edn, Pavilion Publishing, 2019).

Neil Thompson has a long-standing interest in loss and grief issues and their significance across so many aspects of life. His publications on the topic include: *Loss, Grief and Trauma in the Workplace* (Routledge, 2009), *Grief and its Challenges* (Palgrave Macmillan, 2012) and *Handbook of the Sociology of Death, Grief and Bereavement* (co-edited with Gerry Cox, Routledge, 2018). He is a member of the International Work Group on Death, Dying and Bereavement. In 2014 he was presented with the Dr Robert Fulton Award for excellence in the field of death, dying and bereavement at the Center for Death Education and Bioethics at the University of Wisconsin-La Crosse.

About this manual

Who is this manual for?

If…

▶ you are involved in organising and delivering training for a social care, health care, educational or voluntary agency

▶ you are teaching in higher or further education and need or want to deliver a module about either death, dying and bereavement specifically or loss and grief more broadly; or you wish to include sessions about these issues as part of another module (on human growth and development, for example)

▶ you are required to provide training events in industry or any major organisation that seeks to care for its staff in recognition of the importance of workplace well-being

▶ you are involved in human resources activities and you wish to provide events for colleagues to improve their knowledge and awareness

▶ you are a manager and are concerned about how most effectively and sensitively to manage your workforce when issues of loss arise…

and, if …

▶ you want you and your colleagues to find out more about the impact of grief and loss upon your ordinary everyday and work-based lives

Then this training manual could be just right for you!

However…

It is not a manual for training counsellors or other professional colleagues who seek to offer therapeutic help to people whose grief has provoked serious psychological reactions in their lives. In short, this manual will help you to prepare and lead training events that will increase and enhance participants' awareness and understanding. While we do not underestimate the impact of grief and loss upon our lives, we do not want you to think that the subject matter is so specialised that it cannot be handled in a general way as part of an organisation's training strategy.

And so, armed with this manual, you will be able to deliver high-quality, relevant and satisfying training events. You will know that you are able to deliver and, more importantly, you will be able to recognise where specialist help may be required.

Why have we produced this manual?

Directly or indirectly, we all have to cope with the experience of loss almost on a daily basis. Hardly a day goes by without some event taking place which affects us emotionally.

For example:

▶ a child goes missing

▶ people die in a road accident

▶ workers are laid off in a nearby factory

▶ a major public figure dies

▶ someone becomes terminally ill

▶ a company goes into receivership.

The list is endless, and by and large most of us deal with the emotional upset of such events in a variety of ways which enable us to get on with our lives, and, significantly, with our careers and jobs. A quick phone call, text message or email; ten minutes talking with a colleague or friend on the way to work or during a break; a well-practised ability to 'switch off' such concerns and to get on with the job in hand: without such strategies, none of us would function effectively, and our employment would be at risk.

Every now and again, however, the loss is of such significance to us that our normal coping mechanisms cannot deal with it. The loss we are experiencing hits us hard – indeed the very language we use to describe it is revealing:

gutted

pole-axed

knocked sideways

in a daze

bewildered

can't cope

can't think properly

These are the occasions when, for a while at least, life as we know it has changed; when we are not at all sure how to handle things; when we are far from confident in our own ability to cope. It may be that this is the first time we have experienced such a loss, and as a result we will be in uncharted territory – the fact that others may have been in a similar situation does not seem to be particularly helpful or relevant. Suddenly, the everyday tasks which we usually take in our stride become hugely demanding; our feelings well up inside us without prior warning, and we find ourselves apologising for 'being silly'.

We very quickly become aware of the prevailing culture in our workplace towards such issues – the immediate and apparently sympathetic response soon fades, and we get the message that we need to be getting on with the job; that people don't want to be burdened with our problems. 'Take a few days leave to sort yourself out, and then get back to it.'

It may be that men's experiences here are more difficult than women's. Many men still carry the expectation that to be a man, especially a 'macho' man, means to push aside any softer feelings or any admission of weakness or hurt. Crying with joy at scoring a winning goal, or seeing your team clinch the title is acceptable. Tears of weakness, pain, hurt or loss, however, undermine the image which many men have of themselves.

This training manual is therefore designed to help you as a trainer or tutor, and those who attend the courses and events that you organise, to understand better some of these issues and how people react to various losses in their lives. In these days, when many organisations are striving to achieve excellence in their performance as employers – Investors in People-type schemes, and so on – it is important that care is taken to understand how people react to various losses, and how organisations can respond appropriately.

This is not to suggest, however, that companies struggling to survive in a fiercely competitive market should somehow 'go soft' and lose their driving force. Far from it. But it does suggest that responsible employers need to have such issues on their management agendas and in their discussions with trades unions and professional associations, in order to develop appropriate policies and strategies for everyone in the organisation, including managers, when major issues of loss occur in their lives.

There is, of course, a further dimension to this. There are some organisations where life and death issues are almost part of the everyday fabric of the job. Emergency services – police, ambulance crews and fire fighters; and health service personnel – hospital staff, doctors, nurses – all will have constant exposure to grief and loss, often in tragic and sometimes in catastrophic circumstances. In this 'post-September 11th era' we are all so much more conscious of such issues, and the emotional impact such loss can have upon human services practitioners. This training manual has been designed to support trainers who work in such settings.

The list of people affected by sudden loss seems endless. Newspaper and television headlines will highlight briefly the tragic news of a gunman wreaking havoc in a school; of young people and children being kidnapped; of school trips and adventure holidays when tragedy strikes; of major road accidents, train crashes and air disasters; of industrial accidents; of university students, college lecturers, or prisoners committing suicide. The media headlines will soon change, but the emotional devastation and long-term impact of such events has no such brief time scale. People working in these organisations, and especially managers, will have to carry a particularly heavy burden at these times and will often wonder how most sensitively and effectively to support their staff and colleagues. This manual has been designed to support trainers who are called upon to work in such settings.

One further group of people who will encounter such issues as part of their day-to-day work is the armed forces. By definition, members of the armed forces have to be prepared to kill others, both in an individual and in a collective context. They have to be trained to kill in individual combat, and also, for some at least, to press buttons which will result in multiple deaths. In order to be able to fulfil this role, training produces an emotional detachment from the consequences of inflicting loss and grief upon others. There is an inevitable brutalising aspect to this type of work. By contrast, the armed forces pride themselves on the care which they offer to their personnel and recognise that all human beings have their limits beyond which they cannot go. How such organisations deal with issues of grief and loss is particularly important therefore, and much of this manual will provide valuable material for use in such contexts.

Overview of the manual

There is a vast literature available about grief and loss, death, dying and bereavement, and in many ways this manual only scratches the surface of what is available on these subjects. What it does offer you, however, is an accessible introduction to these themes and issues, to help you as a trainer develop sufficient confidence to lead training events in this field to raise people's awareness and understanding. We recognise that many people – including some trainers – feel a bit reticent about these issues. Death, dying, bereavement and loss are not exactly fun topics; they can be a bit 'scary', even when we want to tackle them.

Part One of the manual, *Setting the context*, has therefore been written specifically with you in mind, as a busy trainer or tutor, with perhaps little previous experience of training or teaching in this area. There is a series of fairly short sections setting out some of the issues that will be helpful to you. For example:

▶ What is loss?

▶ What is grief?

▶ What is mourning?

▶ How do people usually cope?

▶ Where do religion and spirituality fit in all of this?

▶ How do different cultures handle these issues?

▶ How can things go wrong?

▶ What can we do to help?

▶ What specialist help is available for you and your workplace?

These sections will set the scene for you as a trainer, to help you feel confident in preparing and leading your training event.

Part Two, *Training and development*, consists of a set of training materials or exercises which you can pick and choose to suit the occasion. Each one has a clear purpose with some suggested things to do to help people get the most out of the event. There are presentation slides which can be downloaded at www.pavpub.com/learning-from-practice-resources, so that your own preparation time can be focused and effective without having to spend time deciding what to put onto slides. Of course, you may wish to add to what we have prepared, which is fine, but we hope that we have provided you with sufficiently detailed materials to run your event successfully.

Part Three, *Conclusion*, serves mainly as a reference section. we have suggested some further reading and have indicated some relevant organisations and websites in case you wish to take issues further.

What should I do next?

This is a crucial question. It is worthwhile spending ten minutes or so trying to answer some of the questions outlined below – this will help you clarify in your own mind why you feel drawn to this training manual and how you might get the best use out of it.

Questions to get you thinking:

▶ What are the particular issues in your organisation which make you think that a training event on 'responding to loss' will be useful and relevant?

▶ What do you hope will be the principal benefits for your organisation from having an event such as this?

▶ What sort of event do you have in mind? A half day? A whole day? Or more?

▶ Who is your 'target audience' for this event?

▶ What do you think will attract your 'target audience' to such an event? What's in it for them? What's in it for the organisation as a whole?

▶ How will you 'sell' the idea to (i) your manager? and (ii) potential participants?

▶ What are the 'put downs' your idea is likely to receive? How will you respond?

▶ What kind of venue will work best for this sort of event?

▶ What budget do you have available to run this event?

▶ What size of group do you think will work best for such an event?

▶ Is there anyone who can help you with the planning and delivery of the event?

▶ If you are a tutor, are you intending to deliver a full module on this subject matter? If so, what topics do you intend to cover and in what order?

It is worthwhile trying to be as clear in your mind as possible about these key questions at the outset. Only you know the exact needs of your organisation and how these materials will be able to help. To do this preparatory thinking now will make your overall planning that much more straightforward and is much more likely to result in a successful event. We would argue that unless you are clear about all the above issues, the success of the training event is likely to be jeopardised. Conversely, if you get this basic planning right, you can feel confident that the materials we provide will not only result in a successful training event, it may well lead to requests for you to organise some more!

This leads us to put the spotlight on you, as a trainer, in a gentle but important way. It is likely, as we have suggested in this introduction, that you will have experienced a range of losses in your life, from relatively trivial ones to perhaps some major losses. You are wanting to lead some courses about 'loss' and it is very important that your own needs do not get in the way. If, for example, you have recently experienced a major loss yourself and you do not feel you have 'got over it' yet; if you are still feeling numb or angry, or confused about it, it is wise not to try to lead a group until you have 'got on top of things' more. This is not something to feel bad about – it is just an acknowledgment that, as trainers or tutors, we need to be able to lead a session competently and effectively and to be aware of other people's needs as the course unfolds. We are less able to do this if a warning bell keeps clanging inside our heads, or we start feeling upset ourselves because of a loss which is still obstinately sitting at the forefront of our minds. We as trainers need time and space for ourselves, just like the rest of the world does!

As a trainer or tutor you would want to say something to anyone wishing to attend the events you are going to lead. Someone who has recently sustained a major loss in their life is probably best advised to delay coming onto your course until they have 'come out the other side' from their stressful feelings. There are people who can give specialised help – bereavement counsellors who have been trained to help people to work through their painful feelings and reactions to loss. You do not want to find yourself in the middle of a training session when a group member suddenly becomes deeply distressed and disrupts the entire flow and timing of the training event.

All of this is a powerful reminder to us that the sort of issues you are going to be dealing with on your training courses, however brief the event may be, can be difficult and upsetting – how could it be otherwise? Loss is rarely easy to deal with. Revisit the list of losses as evidence of that. But human beings can be enormously resilient, and the materials we have provided have been written with these points firmly in mind. We will not be asking you to use materials that are likely to trigger strong reactions in people. Your training events are to raise people's awareness and deepen their knowledge – they are not intended to be group therapy sessions or even emotional support groups for people actively seeking to deal with the impact of recent losses in their lives.

You can be confident, therefore, in using these materials. But you will still need to be honest with yourself about 'where you are coming from'. This is not just about your own experiences of loss, how you have handled them, and the impact they have had on your life. It also involves you being clear about who you are and how this will impact upon your training.

Trainers and tutors are not neutral, any more than authors of training manuals are neutral. As the authors of this manual, we need to acknowledge that we are both white, non-disabled, heterosexual men, one who belongs to a faith community and one who does not. Even this brief self-description will tell you a lot about where we are coming from; about what we can do and, more importantly, what we cannot. Try as we might to empathise with a female perspective, we can never really fully understand. Furthermore, we need to acknowledge that, for many women, the world is shaped and controlled by men who want things to be done their way and who denigrate, and are sometimes violent towards, women. Try as we might to empathise with people of colour, we will never know what it is like to be seen first of all as black – and dismissed, or abused even – because of that. Try as we might to empathise with gay and lesbian people, we are not gay. Try as we might to empathise with disabled people, we can never know what it is like to be without sight, or hearing, or to be mentally unwell, or to be a wheelchair user. Try as we might to wonder what our lives would be like with or without religious faith we still have to acknowledge that it is part and parcel of who we are.

All this is part of our attempt at being honest about where we are coming from, the values we hold, and the capacity we have to discriminate against others. Some would argue, of course, that even in the words we have used in the preceding paragraph about 'trying to empathise' with people different from ourselves, we have been just a touch patronising – and they could be right. For that is a risk we run in regarding our standpoints as the norm against which we judge others.

Journey's end for us, therefore, is the point where we really do celebrate difference; where we value the differing viewpoints and perspectives and lifestyles of others. And this is not a morbid (interesting use of words here!) introspection – it reflects a value base that you as trainer or tutor will need also to own and work from. Otherwise, you run the risk of failing to treat people different from yourself in your training group with integrity and respect.

It is worthwhile therefore – or, rather, we would suggest that it is crucially important – that you spend some time reflecting on 'where you are coming from' as a trainer or tutor, and consider the impact of your experiences upon the training you hope to deliver – whether this is as male or female; straight or gay; disabled or non-disabled; white or a person of colour; and so on. Who you really are will come across in the training, whether you realise it or not.

The good news, of course, is that if you are able to do this, you have the potential to be a really effective trainer or tutor in an area where the need is great. It is worthwhile, therefore, to undertake this preparatory work so that both you and the course participants get the most out of your training events.

Part One:
Setting the context

What is loss?

This seemingly obvious question underpins this entire training manual, and so it is important to tackle it at the outset. It should be clear to you already from the Introduction to this manual that we are taking a very broad view about loss, rather than limiting it to the potentially emotionally traumatic issues of death and bereavement.

The reason for this is not to diminish the importance of death and bereavement – far from it. But they are the very obvious examples of loss, where organisations and managers frequently have a clear policy and strategy for dealing with people in such situations. Compassionate leave is now enshrined in best practice, although there remains considerable variation from work sector to work sector and organisation to organisation.

But loss is much more varied. It affects us in far more ways than perhaps we realise. Significantly, the range of feelings we experience in the 'big losses', such as in bereavement, may be felt with varying degrees of intensity in the smaller losses. They may affect our capacity to cope and to deal with our everyday responsibilities; they may get in the way of our relationships, and cause all manner of people to wonder 'what's up with him or her?' We may feel 'out of sorts', and not realise that these feelings are due to the loss we are experiencing. It is important to be aware of these basic issues that can have a serious impact upon our working lives, as well as our private moments.

One of the exercises that we suggest for your training event in Part Two of the manual is called 'Listing the losses'. The purpose is very simple: it encourages us to take as broad a view as possible about how loss can affect us. Everyone will have their own list, of course, and it is important to stress that there are no wrong answers – if something feels like a loss for someone, then it is a loss, whether or not other people recognise it. Some people, for example, may laugh at the news that someone's pet hamster has died. But if, for the owner, that hamster was a precious part of their lives, of course its death will be felt acutely.

For the purposes of illustration only, there follows a list of losses (apart from being bereaved when someone close to you dies) which is far from exhaustive, and is not in any particular order, but seeks to illustrate the wide range of loss. You may find it helpful to use it as a checklist for this exercise when you do it 'for real':

▶ divorce or separation from a partner

▶ loss of physical capacity through accidents

▶ loss of earning power

▶ loss of self-esteem and confidence

▶ loss of virility and sexual potency

▶ loss through theft or burglary

▶ loss of employment – redundancy, for example

▶ physical illness

▶ loss of hearing or losing your sight

▶ friends moving out of the area

▶ children moving from home – getting married, going to college

▶ loss of familiar surroundings when you move house

▶ losses on the stock market – pension funds, profits

▶ loss of reputation and one's good name

▶ losing a sense of purpose in life

▶ loss of one's mental and intellectual capacities

▶ having your car stolen – or your wallet or handbag snatched

▶ losing your religious faith

▶ loss of professional identity following retirement

▶ losing your belongings while on holiday

▶ losing your clean driving licence – penalty points, disqualification

▶ losing your bedding plants to a sharp frost

▶ losing a small fortune at the bookies

▶ losing your good looks

▶ loss of dignity

▶ losses that follow from being assaulted or raped

▶ loss of sobriety as a result of 'problem drinking'

▶ losing the feeling of safety and security because your partner is violent

▶ losing your independence.

This list of losses is not meant to make you feel depressed, though it easily could… Instead, it is intended to illustrate how all-pervasive loss can be in our lives. It reminds us vividly that all of us have to cope with the experience of loss almost on a daily basis. However the impact which these losses have upon us depends to a large degree on their significance to us.

For example, we used the scenario of a person losing heavily at the bookies in our list. To a hardened gambler, this could perhaps be dismissed fairly lightly, with the long-term view of 'win some, lose some – there's always tomorrow'. If, by contrast, it was someone desperate to gain some cash to avert a crisis, and who gambled a whole month's housekeeping money and then lost the lot, that could have a catastrophic impact upon them emotionally, not to mention the reception awaiting them at home. If, however, it was someone who was already seriously addicted to gambling, it would point up even more starkly the need for skilled professional help.

It would be an interesting exercise – indeed you may wish to use this with your group when you run your training event – to revisit this list of losses, and to ask yourself what impact each of these would have upon you. Some of them would probably be brushed aside with little or no difficulty because they didn't 'get to you' in any way. There will be others, however, where you genuinely do not know how you would cope – they seem so awful that you cannot imagine being anything other than overwhelmed by them. These are the 'big losses' as far as you are concerned, which may or may not chime in with other people's 'big losses'. No matter – if they are 'big' for you, and have a profound effect upon your emotional and maybe physical well-being, they need to be taken seriously. People who belong to a faith community, for example, may well feel that the loss of their faith would turn their whole world upside down; to someone for whom religious faith was not important, however, this could seem an extraordinarily unnecessary state for someone to get themselves into.

Setting the context

In considering your list of losses, there will be some for which you will have to be held responsible – if you drove through the speed camera too fast, or chose to drive under the influence of alcohol, then the loss of your clean licence, a fair amount of money by way of a fine, and maybe a disqualification can only be attributed to you and the choices you made on that particular occasion. Kick yourself you may, but to kick others instead would be a trifle unfair on them.

Far more difficult to cope with are the losses over which you have no control. If someone close to you is seriously injured or even killed by a drunken driver; if a close friend or partner develops a life-threatening illness for which there is no cure; if the company in which you invested heavily suddenly goes into bankruptcy, then you could be sent reeling from the impact of an event over which you had no control whatsoever.

It is often these feelings of helplessness – of events being out of our control – that make the impact of certain losses far harder to bear. It won't stop us trying to blame someone, of course, but often the finger of blame wavers uncertainly, and we are left feeling infinitely worse: angry, hurt, resentful.

With the examples we have given, highly selective though they are, it is likely that other people will acknowledge, to a greater or lesser degree, what we are going through. They will know something about it from their own experience, and there may be some degree of comfort received from that 'comradeship of suffering'. Even if it is not hugely helpful to have someone tell you how it was for them when they went through a similar experience, at least it locates your experience in territory which others too sometimes share. You don't feel totally different, or outcast, because of your loss.

It is worth noting, however, that for some people there are losses which cannot be publicly acknowledged or owned. The very fact of acknowledging the loss is itself an act of 'giving the game away' – something that carries greater risks than remaining silent about one's loss. The formal name for this is 'disenfranchised grief', and it refers to a very difficult and painful situation.

Three examples will illustrate what is meant by this.

First, imagine that you are having an affair with someone who is married to someone else. You have been seeing each other for some time, and you only really feel happy when you are together. You plan to move in together as soon as you can. But then suddenly, before the news of your affair has been shared, your lover is killed in a car crash. You are devastated – but who can you tell? Those who are involved in the immediate family know nothing; they plan the funeral; they receive the sympathy; they have people to talk to. You, by contrast, are left holding a dreadful secret, and a pain you cannot divulge. You are outside the 'normal' circle – disenfranchised.

Second, many people who are gay feel unable to 'come out' in any public or semi-public way about their sexual orientation or about their partner. Some societies can still be very homophobic, and many gay people fear for their physical safety. A few enter into heterosexual marriages where they remain unhappy and unfulfilled, but at least it gives a cloak of respectability in an otherwise hostile society. Some gay people, of course, do feel able to live openly and freely with their partners and enjoy the benefit of entering into a civil partnership or same-sex marriage, but for a sizeable number of people this may still seem impossible. Consequently, when their partner dies, they feel unable to acknowledge or own their feelings in any public way.

Their lover's family may not have known anything about their sexual orientation and will go ahead with the funeral arrangements. The best that the gay person, who possibly feels the loss most acutely, can hope for is to slip into the back of the funeral event, and grieve unnoticed. He or she is outside the 'normal circle' – disenfranchised.

Third, a woman who finds that she is pregnant and who decides, for whatever reason, that she will seek an abortion without telling anyone at all about it, has to go through the entire process by herself. The only people who know will be the various healthcare professionals involved in the abortion, but if she were to opt for a 'back street' abortion, then such support would be an absolute minimum. For her, the journey back to her everyday life involves holding a secret and a loss that is unknown to anyone else – indeed, even to acknowledge what she has done would be to run the risks of disapproval which she clearly prefers to avoid. She finds herself outside the 'normal circle' – disenfranchised.

One author who has written about this gives the following definition of disenfranchised grief:

> 'Disenfranchised grief refers to grief that is experienced when a loss cannot be openly acknowledged, socially sanctioned or publicly mourned. There is no perceived "right to grieve".'
> (Doka, 1989)

It is important to give due emphasis to disenfranchised grief, not just because it is probably far more common than we realise, but because as a trainer you will need to handle it sensitively on your courses. You need to raise it, but you also need to recognise that there may be members of your group who feel disenfranchised and who will not wish to disclose the nature of their loss. (You may yourself, as a trainer or tutor, be in a similar position, of course.) It will be important not to compromise their integrity, or to structure a session in such a way that people, whose losses are by definition unknown to you, are not put under pressure in any way.

Having explored some of the complexities of loss, we now turn to a consideration of what is meant by grief.

What is grief?

'Give sorrow words: the grief that does not speak Whispers the o'er-fraught heart, and bids it break.'
(Shakespeare, Macbeth Act 4. sc. 3. line 209)

'Grief: intense sorrow or mental suffering resulting from loss.'
(Webster's Dictionary)

Shakespeare's invitation to give voice to the deep feelings we experience when we suffer loss is both wise advice and also an almost impossible task.

We all recognise that to bottle feelings up is to run the risk of even greater emotional distress in the short, medium or even long term. But the attempt to put these feelings into words can require enormous effort.

It is important to acknowledge this at the outset, however obvious the point may be. If we experience a loss of something or someone who gives meaning and purpose and enjoyment and fulfilment to our lives, the emotional pain we experience will inevitably be intense, even unspeakable.

Consider these phrases:

▶ A living hell.

▶ An empty void.

▶ An aching chasm.

▶ Torn apart.

▶ Utter despair.

▶ Unable to carry on.

▶ Desperately afraid.

These are frequently heard on the lips of people experiencing the sharp awfulness of grief. They are feelings which no one else is able ever to get inside, no matter how sympathetic they try to be.

It is no surprise, therefore, that we often turn to poets on such occasions, for they have a gift with words which others lack. Auden's poignant poem, 'Funeral Blues', used famously in the film 'Four Weddings and a Funeral', expresses it so well (WH Auden, *Tell Me the Truth About Love: Fifteen Poems*, Faber, 1991).

Grief can be raw and full of energy, as well as being at times silent and withdrawn. It is as difficult to talk about as trying to capture clouds in a jam jar. And yet, unless we can find a common language to talk about such things, we will be stifled and helpless, and unable to reach out to anyone who is grieving. Unless we have some understanding of the music and the dance steps of grief, we will be unable to tune in or draw anywhere near to those who are caught up in its discords and unaccustomed swirlings.

The rest of Part One will therefore introduce you to some of these dance steps of grief. It is important to have some grasp of the ways in which people who have spent their professional lives working with grieving people have tried to understand and discover patterns to their behaviours. Some of the dances will perhaps be familiar to you already, others will be new, but each of them in their own way helps us understand something of the complexity of this raw emotion to which we give the name 'grief'.

A word of caution at the outset: these ways of understanding grief – which we have chosen to call 'dances' in this part – are descriptive rather than prescriptive. In other words, they are not hard and fast rules or patterns of behaviour that every grieving person must somehow copy for fear of 'getting it wrong'. On the contrary: every person who grieves will always grieve in the way and style that suits them best. We are our own experts in this field, even if we have never danced this particular lonely dance before.

But it is often helpful to know something of the dance steps we are likely to have to take, if only for the reassurance that the dance will come to some sort of conclusion, sooner or later, and that other (maybe shared) dances will be possible for us after that. It is also helpful to know that if we find ourselves constantly repeating one particular dance step – if we find ourselves getting 'stuck' in a particular corner for whatever reason – we may need some help to explore other parts of the dance floor, and to know that help is available.

The exercises that we offer for your training or teaching sessions will make it clear that there are no 'right or wrong' theories about grieving: some people may find more help in one approach, others may prefer an alternative route. As the facilitator, you will need to help people feel comfortable with this variety.

In the sections which follow, you will find that some authors talk about 'stages' through which people pass when grieving; others talk about 'processes'. The idea of 'tasks' of grief has been put forward, alongside the notion of trying to reconstruct a sense of meaning and purpose in our lives after a major loss.

The discussion which follows has been kept brief enough to give you the feel of each approach so that you can use them in your training sessions. Inevitably, some approaches have been left out, and, in the final part of the manual, some wider reading is suggested in order to help you explore issues in further depth, should you wish to do so (and we would certainly encourage you to so, as there is so much to be learned about these important but complex issues).

There is one further point that needs to be made. A lot of the work that has been undertaken in this field has had a white European 'feel' to it. There is a danger, however, that we may assume that what may fit one cultural background will automatically fit all cultural groups. This is an issue that we explore later in this manual, but it is important to begin reflecting on this issue at the outset. We need to develop a multicultural and multi-faith sensitivity to these issues, and you may well find in your sessions that group members may enrich the sessions with their own cultural understanding and experiences. But as a facilitator, you will need to raise this issue with the group, and we have provided some exercise material to help you do this.

Approach 1: The Dual Process model

A very good starting place for our understanding of how people grieve is a relatively new 'dance' that has been called the 'dual process' model. Like so many other people working in this field, its authors (Margaret Stroebe and Henk Schut) noticed that many people who experience profound loss have a remarkable ability to do two things at once. We may best illustrate this with an example.

Picture a woman who has been recently bereaved. She is at home by herself, in emotional turmoil. She is distressed, disorientated, pottering aimlessly about the house. Suddenly the doorbell rings. Drying her eyes, adjusting her hair and face, she opens the door and deals with having to sign for a package brought by the postal service. Back indoors, she gets on with some household chores – gets upset – and then the phone rings. Putting on a 'brave face' she takes the call, and deals with it in a calm and efficient way.

And so her day, and her week, and her months go by. At times she is distraught; on other occasions she is 'more like her normal self' and can get on with things in a practical way. She has good days and bad days.

She is not alone in this, for it is a common experience for many people who are grieving. Stroebe and Schut have called this the 'dual process' model, because they suggest that all grieving people deal with two quite different processes at one and the same time. The first involves all the horrible feelings which have been stirred up by the loss which has been experienced. At every turn, the person is faced with the implications of their loss – it is LOSS in capital letters and there is no getting away from it. The second is what is often called 'getting on with the rest of your life', or 'restoration', as Stroebe and Schut describe it. It involves all the 101 things that still need to be done, but also moves into the different ways of living which slowly become possible as a new future is faced.

The important thing about this way of understanding is that these two aspects of living – or 'orientations' as Stroebe and Schut call them – go along side by side, and grieving people move from one to the other and back again on a regular basis. In the early days they are likely to be much more in the loss aspect, with occasional moments in the restoration aspect. But as time goes by the balance shifts, and at some point a person will find that far more time is being spent with a future focus as they get on with their lives. But – and it is a big but – there will always be moments, often unguarded, when they find themselves back in the loss aspect – feeling the loss. Key dates like birthdays will often trigger these feelings, and it may take many years before their sharpness diminishes.

In this way of looking at the grief and loss, we should expect there to be times and occasions when the grieving person is upset and 'down in the dumps' – it is natural, and perhaps should even be welcomed as a reminder of the ways in which life was enhanced and enriched by the person who has now died.

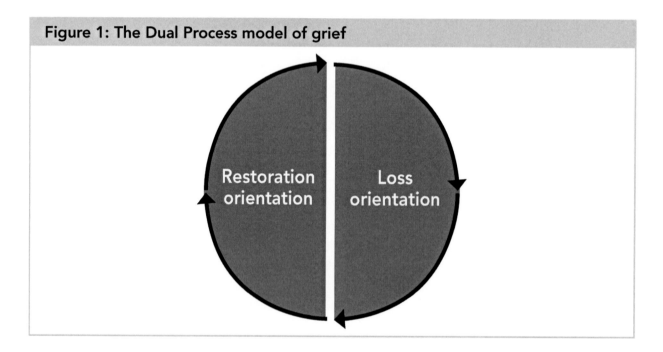

Figure 1: The Dual Process model of grief

Restoration orientation

Loss orientation

Approach 2: The idea of stages

Without doubt, this approach is the one most likely to be quoted by a wide range of people, including many professionals, when asked about how people deal with grief and loss. It owes its origin to Elizabeth Kübler-Ross, who worked as a psychiatrist for many years with dying and bereaved people, but similar approaches have been suggested by other equally eminent practitioners such as John Bowlby and Colin Murray Parkes (see Part Three on p91 of the manual for details of relevant literature).

This approach was based on observations of many dying and bereaved people, where some common themes were noted. These included:

▶ **Denial:** an immediate reaction to the news of someone's death is the refusal to believe it is true – it can't have happened.

- **Numbness:** part of the denial – people can draw into themselves with the shock of bad news – feelings can be too painful so we 'shut down' and refuse to allow ourselves to hurt.

- **Anger:** feelings begin to tumble out of us, without any clear focus or direction – we hurt more than we can say, and we lash out with our tongues at anyone and everyone.

- **Depression:** the anger gets turned in on ourselves – we feel we cannot cope – we may even feel suicidal – life feels not worth living without our loved one.

- **Acceptance:** we 'come to terms' with our loss and begin to rebuild our lives and face a new future.

This is a very basic description of the stages through which a grieving person is said to pass, and more recently this basic model has been expanded to make it more comprehensive and detailed, and also refined to make it feel less mechanistic.

Many of the 'stages' ring bells with a lot of people who can identify with the feelings. Some people find it a comfort that one stage seems to lead to another and that it is a way of reassuring people that there is a 'light at the end of the tunnel'.

It needs to be said, however, that there is now a growing consensus among contemporary writers that involves rejecting even a sophisticated 'stages model', because they feel that it does not do justice to the complexity and variety of people's reactions to grief and loss and runs the risk of being seen as a prescriptive model.

It has also been argued that it is misleading and highly problematic to see depression as in inherent stage of grief. Writers such as Schneider (2012) have pointed out that grieving can appear like depression – the two look superficially similar – but in reality the two are very different things. He argues that failing to distinguish between grieving and depression can mean that many people will be wrongly diagnosed as having depression and therefore given inappropriate (and potentially counterproductive) help. To distinguish between the two it can be helpful to: (i) think of grief as a painful, exhausting and frightening process, but it is a positive process in so far as it involves healing; and (ii) recognise depression as a form of being emotionally 'stuck', as if paralysed. That is, the former involves emotional *movement*, albeit an extremely difficult movement, while the latter involves emotional stasis or lack of movement.

Approach 3: The tasks of grief

Another way of helping us understand what grief is all about was offered by William Worden (2009), who moved away from the idea of stages or processes. He suggested that a helpful way to understand what grief is all about is to identify a number of tasks which a grieving person would need successfully to complete in order to move into the future.

The word 'tasks' may be a little off putting at first – it is not like having a list of jobs to do, like going shopping, paying the rent or doing your washing. Worden has much more psychological tasks in mind, which is hardly surprising as he was deeply involved in grief counselling and issues in people's mental health. He identifies four main areas where, if you like, work has to be done if grief is to be successfully tackled.

▶ **Task One:** To accept the reality of the loss.

▶ **Task Two:** To work through the pain of grief.

▶ **Task Three:** To adjust to a world without the deceased (externally, internally and spiritually).

▶ **Task Four:** To move on emotionally.

It is important to recognise that these are not strictly sequential: it is not a case that you cannot tackle Task Three until Tasks One and Two have been thoroughly accomplished – far from it. For many people it takes a long, long time before Task One is achieved and, maybe for some, it is never finally complete. Some people are caught up into Task Two immediately; others find that it takes a long time before they really let the pain of the event find full expression.

So these are almost parallel tasks, except that Task Four makes it clear that, until some measure of 'letting go' has been achieved, it will be difficult to get on with life. However, Worden also recognises this is more of an adaptation, and that 'eventually moving on' may also involve keeping an enduring connection or continuing bond with the deceased. There are some people for whom this is particularly difficult, as we shall see later, and who need skilled help to complete this particular task.

For many people, the usefulness of this approach is that it highlights the importance of our being involved and seeking to take charge, to some extent at least, of what is happening to us. Although there will be times when we sit back and let things swamp us and overcome us, we will need to find the energy to tackle these tasks, knowing that there is a different future ahead over which we have some control.

Approach 4: Finding new meanings

A common strand running through a lot of people's experience of grief is the loss of any meaning and purpose as a result of their great loss. They had vested so much in this particular relationship that its destruction shattered that sense of meaning for them.

That this is a key theme is beyond doubt, not least because without some sense of meaning and purpose most of us find it difficult to get on with our lives. This is not to propose that there are necessarily grand overarching themes that can give meaning and purpose to our lives. That is something which your course members may wish to debate. At an individual level, however, most of us find something of this sense of meaning and purpose through particular relationships, and when these cease, we find ourselves struggling to find a way forward without them.

This links with both the fourth task identified by Worden, and with another set of approaches that focus on this issue of meaning. Some of the language of previous approaches had been that of 'working through' one's grief; of being able to 'let go' and 'move on' – all of which resonate to some extent with people's experience of grief and loss.

Some more recent approaches, however, encourage more of a narrative or 'story telling' approach which seeks not so much to leave things behind, as to reshape our understanding of where we are, and who we are, in the light of the loss we have experienced. Many bereaved people will talk of their loved one still being with them many years after their physical death. For some, of course, this has a spiritual dimension because of a particular religious faith. But others, without this spirituality, still talk of their lives being influenced by the memory of their loved one; of the 'gap still being very much there' in their lives, which nothing can fill.

Writers who have been exploring this aspect of grieving are now talking about 'story telling' in the sense of reshaping the sense of meaning and purpose after a significant loss. 'Meaning reconstruction' for example, is a phrase used by Robert Neimeyer and his colleagues in the United States (Neimeyer & Anderson, 2002); and Tony Walter in the UK emphasises the importance of retelling the story of the loved one so that it has contemporary significance (Walter, 1999). There is something in the 'reshaping of the biography of the deceased' which releases it from the past and makes it part of our present. 'Getting over a loss', from this perspective, is less a product of counselling or 'treatment' and much more a creative, albeit painful reshaping of our individual world in the aftermath of the loss.

We have covered a lot of ground so far in this section – and it may be that even such a sketchy introduction has left you feeling a little bewildered, and also wondering about the right way to proceed. The message we would like to leave with you at this stage is that contemporary understandings of grief and loss are suggesting that there is no single, correct way to approach these issues. There is a wide variety of ways in which people express their loss and seek to deal with it. This can be enormously liberating, and we hope that you as a trainer or tutor will be able to use our materials in such a way as to convey this sense of adventure, almost, as people discover the right way for them to handle such complex issues.

What is mourning?

In a crude sense, if grief is what we feel when we experience loss, mourning is what we do to express it. Grief may well be unique to each individual; to mourning, however, there will be some common themes and patterns, not least because how we express our grief is controlled to no small extent by the society we live in and the norms which are somehow agreed by that society to be acceptable. There is therefore a strong sociological dimension to mourning.

As an example of this, compare a 'white European' funeral event with a similar event in, say, India or the Middle East. The one tends to be somewhat formal, 'dignified' (whatever is meant by that), focused on family and friends, and emotionally restrained; the other tends to be more community-oriented, emotionally charged and overflowing with tears, with at times almost an 'explosion' of grief.

That last paragraph was written, inescapably, from a white European perspective, and illustrates how difficult it is to stand outside your own experience and values and 'report upon another cultural perspective'. Someone reporting on a white European funeral event might well feel that it is a very uninvolved, detached and unsatisfactory way of mourning. This is something you may wish to discuss with people in your training event.

Within contemporary Western societies, however, we have strong multicultural traditions which help us understand again that there is no single right way of mourning. Societies and cultures develop their own rituals and patterns of behaviour which somehow are felt to meet the needs of those taking part.

Not that such rituals are unchangeable. It will be interesting to see what your group members' experience is of how things have changed over the last decades in the UK. Gone are some of the outward vestiges of mourning – the dark clothes; the drawn curtains; the black armbands worn for several months. People attending funerals no longer feel that showing respect has to be equated with wearing black or dark-coloured clothing, although here again the multicultural dimension to our society has made an impact.

By contrast, we have seen other rituals being introduced. Flowers placed by the roadside or tied to the railings to mark the place where someone has died is one example. In some ways the death of Princess Diana may have been a turning point in the mourning behaviour of the people in the UK – the sheer vastness of the ocean of flowers and the number of people attending the event took it into a different league from many other national mournings. Paradoxically however, our experience of such events has become more and more dominated by the decisions taken by the media, especially television, for which (we may suppose) some good close-up shots of people in floods of tears make for better viewing than lines of sombre-faced observers. The impact of the media's coverage of Princess Diana's funeral also provided something of a benchmark for subsequent large-scale events, with the observation that 'there weren't as many flowers as for Diana', for example, carrying the implication that 'people cannot be feeling as deeply as they did then'.

These are complex issues to discuss, but the principal point we wish to make is that how we mourn is often controlled, or certainly heavily influenced, by society's norms and expectations. Maybe this is because we are afraid of the powerful feelings which grief releases in us, and we feel the need for a safe channel for us to be guided along. So we take it for granted that funeral directors will tell us what to do at every step along the way and will 'get it right' on our behalf. We take it for granted that there will be professionals at hand to conduct the funeral event, either within our particular faith community, or from a secular, humanist perspective. Such 'experts' will tell us what to do and how to do it – they will explain how such things are managed so that we can 'do it properly'.

All this has led some commentators to observe that all our mourning is (to use Walter's words) 'regulated, controlled, patrolled, policed' (1999, p120). Not that this is intended to be a negative criticism; it highlights, rather, the ways in which all societies have certain expectations about how to handle death, and how those who are bereaved are expected to behave, certainly in the public domain.

The significance of 'ritual'

We have used the word 'ritual' several times already, and it is worth spending a little time reflecting on why rituals are important. They are not restricted to religious events, although faith communities do place great significance on a wide range of rituals to help people engage with key elements of their faith. In a wider sense, however, rituals surrounding bereavement in particular – such as funeral and memorial events – are judged to be important for people to participate in at key moments of loss because they bring into focus several key themes. These include:

▶ *the reality of the loss* – the ritual is a stark bringing into focus of the reality of the loss. Some cultures will seek to have this event within 24 hours, while for others it may be over a week following the death.

▶ *the sense of community* – this will have both family and community dimensions to remind us that often a wide number of people will mourn this person.

▶ *a sense of continuity* – the ritual is a formal expression of the continuity of the family and community and a commitment to continuing the work of the person who is being mourned. That person, in one, will 'live on' in the work which the community continues to fulfil.

▶ *maintaining contacts* – rituals are also occasions for maintaining and renewing links between family and community members.

▶ *'re-learning the world'* – Attig's (2010) powerful phrase is apt, in that rituals help people to rehearse and rewrite the new family or community story following their bereavement.

How do people deal with grief and loss?

One of the most difficult aspects of this area of human behaviour is the sheer complexity and variety in people's responses to loss and the ways in which they choose to grieve and mourn. We have already indicated that society has ways of channelling and controlling how we mourn through the various rituals and traditions we observe. At the individual level, however, there are also some commonly understood guidelines about how best to cope with such unsettling and unnerving experiences, not all of which are always necessarily helpful.

It is much more commonplace today than in the 19th century, for example, to recognise the significance of expressing our feelings more openly. It is felt generally that to 'bottle feelings up' can lead to psychologically damaging problems later. 'Better out than in;

sooner rather than later; and get it out of your system as soon as you can' is a rather crude summary of popular wisdom about expressing our feelings of grief.

But what right have we to prescribe how people should feel and behave? The pervasive influence of the 'stages' models of grieving has led some well-meaning professionals and lay people alike to voice some expectations about how people should be feeling at such and such a 'stage' of their grieving process'. And if the individual's experience does not fit the professional view, they tend to feel that they are 'doing it wrong' and perhaps even feel guilty as a result.

Another assumption which is also pervasive suggests that women and men must surely grieve 'in the same way', and that if men refuse or are unable to do it in the same way as women, they are at fault and are storing up problems for themselves. There are, admittedly, some stereotypical behaviours and responses to serious loss portrayed in our television soaps, with women getting emotionally distraught in floods of tears, while the men 'go quiet' and resort to lashings of alcohol to drown their sorrows before giving vent to anger.

It is dangerous to make such assumptions, but it is also misleading to suggest that men and women alike must always react and respond in similar ways. At the root of the issue may well be the question of meaning which we have already discussed, together with the sense of attachment which women and men feel to the person who has died, or from whom they have been divorced. The stronger the bond between them, the greater is likely to be the sense of loss which is felt. But, if some people choose not to reveal their feelings – and it may be that more men come into this category than women – does this give us the right to say that they are not 'doing it properly'? This is something you may well wish to discuss with the members of your group.

Given this variety of responses, however, it is nevertheless helpful to have some idea about some of the feelings and behaviours which characterise people who experience loss. It can be useful for managers and colleagues at work to be aware of what people who are grieving may be going through, so that they can respond appropriately.

The list that follows is intended to be illustrative – to give you some 'for instances' of the sort of ways in which grief affects people. Even so, it will not make easy reading – but experiencing profound loss is not easy either, so it should come as no surprise to us that people find it difficult to keep on an even keel. Nor are all the reactions straightforward – sometimes there are conflicting emotions to deal with, which makes it even harder for everyone.

Some of the feelings may include:

▶ panic

▶ fear

▶ vulnerability

▶ anger

- guilt
- loneliness
- despair
- hopelessness
- hostility
- 'going mad'
- relief
- pining
- irritability
- impatience
- being overwhelmed.

Some of the things people do may include:

- withdrawing socially
- becoming restless and overactive
- becoming accident-prone or careless
- searching for the deceased
- crying a lot
- wanting not to be left alone
- drinking a lot
- seeking out sexual partners
- losing concentration.

Some of the physical aspects people experience may include:

- fatigue
- lethargy
- nervousness
- dizziness
- chest pains
- back ache

▶ tummy upsets

▶ finding it hard to swallow

▶ fainting

▶ dry mouth

▶ sweating

▶ cold, clammy hands

▶ inability to sleep properly.

It is a formidable list, and in the literature there are many more physical aspects given to illustrate how painful, disorientating and debilitating grief can be. To be aware of this, of course, can in itself be a comfort to people who are grieving, provided that we seek mainly to listen rather than to judge or advise (the impact of grief can be so intense that people can feel that they are going mad, so being made aware that what they are experiencing is a natural reaction can be very helpful to them). Nor should we attempt to offer medical advice – people who are grieving frequently need professional medical help, even if only for a short time, to help them sleep, for example. The crucial issue for workplace colleagues and managers, however, is to have sufficient awareness to assess whether a person is capable of undertaking their work tasks satisfactorily, or whether they are putting themselves or others at risk. This will depend on circumstances: some people will find going to work an enormous comfort and help in the process of rebuilding their lives – remember the 'dual process' approach to grief and loss outlined earlier.

Perhaps the hardest but most important thing other people can do is simply to be there for the person who is experiencing the loss; to offer the caring hand; the listening ear; to represent the sheer ordinariness and boring routine of daily living, work-based banter and gossip; of including rather than cold shouldering out of embarrassment; to let them talk if they want to, but to be relaxed about it if they don't. Ordinary though this may seem, it can make all the difference in the world.

Religion and spirituality

For many people, the experience of loss, and particularly bereavement, brings them in touch with a lot of issues that are in the territory of religion and spirituality, whether or not they themselves belong to a faith community. This is mainly because, as we have noted already, issues of loss raise basic questions of meaning and purpose in our lives, questions to which most religions seek to offer some kind of response.

It would be an impossibly ambitious task in this short overview to seek to tackle the whole range of religions and approaches to spirituality, and it would be counterproductive for such a training course as you are planning. There is all the difference in the world between learning facts about a particular religion and yourself being part of that faith community. The same holds true for spirituality, which is a term that faith communities recognise and own, but also applies to a much wider range of experiences that point people to a 'deeper' or 'higher' dimension to human existence, and which enables many people to come up with some responses to the question about meaning and purpose to life.

One of the characteristics of the monotheistic religions – that is, those who have a belief in the Oneness of a Divine Being, such as Christianity, Islam and Judaism – is that there is a belief in an afterlife for the essential spirit or soul of the individual believer. For those who belong to these faith communities, therefore, questions about meaning and purpose need to be seen in the much wider context of a life after death. Their sense of loss will be tempered, to some extent at least, with the faith that their loved one 'lives on' in a spiritual plane. Other religions share a belief in reincarnation and believe that the quality of the life we live determines whether we shall return in a 'higher' or 'lower' life form after we die. There are others who believe that there is something of the divine not only in each and every person but in every aspect of the physical world as well.

We have begun to indicate something of the complexity of this topic, and if you wish to discover more about this there are a wide range of books and websites you can explore. For the purpose of this course material, however, we do not suggest that you need to be any more of an expert than you already are in this field. By which we mean that, whether or not you belong to a faith community, whether or not you 'own' a specific approach to spirituality, whether or not you have for yourself a clearly defined response to the big questions about meaning and purpose in life, you will have your own personal integrity as an individual and as a trainer. This will involve you being open to other people's ideas, experiences, beliefs and opinions, and a willingness to explore the implications of these approaches to the issues of loss.

We have accordingly adopted a general approach to these issues in our training materials, so that they can be as widely applicable to all your course members. We hope, nonetheless, that you as a trainer will give some prior thought to these issues and where you stand, so that you can be as open and enabling as possible when you are leading your sessions.

Exploring different cultures

We have already stressed the significance of the multicultural nature of society in the UK: and this is not just in some of the more visibly obvious ways with black and Asian and Chinese communities, for example. Our cultural heritage is both complex and intertwined: different parts of the UK celebrate their cultural differences in all sorts of ways, and sometimes have different approaches to various aspects of life. The sense of belonging to a community is much stronger in some areas than in, for example, large cities, though even here there can be close-knit groups with a strong sense of belonging. We also experience differences in other ways. Within the wider population, for example, there are those who take deep pride in being deaf, who do not wish to be regarded as disabled but who have a deep sense of being able to celebrate their difference and specialness, and who present a challenge to the hearing world which so often excludes them.

Similar comments might be made for visually impaired people, those with learning difficulties, those who regularly use wheelchairs, people with mental health problems, and many more. The world as they experience it often discriminates against them and excludes them from mainstream events and experiences, and also frequently fails to take into account their needs when they experience grief and loss.

The main message here is similar to the one given in the previous section about religious and spiritual diversity. Cultural diversity is part of the fabric of our society and includes far more dimensions than those that are immediately obvious. It would be impossible for any trainer to be knowledgeable about all these complex issues – and again it would be inappropriate. What we suggest is important is that in our training we foster a particular set of values – a particular way of approaching these issues.

This approach is often called 'valuing diversity', and this, we suggest, is fundamental to your training courses. It is certainly the value base of the training materials in this manual. It involves your bringing a spirit of honest enquiry and openness to your training sessions; of recognising that different cultural groups may well have their own special ways of responding to grief and loss, and have particular rituals and observances which encourage and enable the members of their group to handle such experiences. Such rituals and observances may not suit you, they may not suit other people you know, but if they work for a particular cultural group and are important to them, we must recognise and respect them for this, and not attempt to make other people fit into our ways of doing things.

There are books and materials available for people to consult about different cultural perspectives on grief and loss, but, as far as this manual is concerned, it is much more important to get the message across of valuing diversity than trying to give you potted versions of how other people deal with these issues.

One of the best places to start, therefore, is with your own experience and your own cultural background, and to use the materials provided as a way in to celebrate both your own and other group members' cultural distinctiveness. In that way, everyone in the group will feel valued, and will have a contribution to make.

Grief: How can things go wrong? Difficult and complicated grieving

Had this manual been written a few decades ago, it would have been much easier to write. There was then a much clearer delineation between 'normal' and 'abnormal' grief, and it was possible to write from a clinical perspective on a range of things which could go wrong for people in grief.

While it is undoubtedly true that some people's grieving takes them into the depths of despair, depression and even mental instability for which skilled professional help is needed, the demarcation between styles and patterns of grieving is now far less clearly defined. This follows logically from the position we have been describing in these sections: if we now have come to realise that each and every person will find their own way of dealing with and expressing their grief, then there is no longer a clear pattern, or timetable even, for people's mourning. Consequently, someone taking twice as long as someone else to reach a position where they feel able to get on with the rest of their lives fairly confidently need not be pathologised or described as somehow inadequate, or in need of psychiatric help. It is simply the case that, for them, a different time frame is operating: they are doing it 'their way'.

That having been said, there can be particular difficulties which some people may experience for which skilled professional help is needed. We have already mentioned some of these, such as deep depression, which is a serious condition that can be addressed through skilled professional help.

There are some indicators, however, that grieving may be more complicated in some situations than others. As you might expect, these are given technical names in the literature, but behind these names lie some very real and painful experiences.

'Chronic grief', for example, describes a situation where someone really does seem to be stuck in the grieving process, and seems genuinely unable to make any progress at all. For some people this can last for months, years even: Queen Victoria is often cited as an example of this.

By contrast, 'absent grief' is a term used to describe someone who has sustained a serious loss but then seems to carry on as if nothing has happened. It needs to be said that people who react in this way can sometimes be caught off their guard with another, maybe far less serious loss, some months or even years later, and then the cumulative grief reactions almost explode, and seem far more serious than the second event would seem to demand. This is called 'delayed grief' and can be very disabling.

People's grief may be made more complicated by the circumstances of their loss which can often exacerbate their grief. A few examples will serve to illustrate this:

▶ Violent and messy deaths – for example, murder or road accidents.

▶ Multiple losses – for example, death plus divorce or redundancy.

▶ Sudden deaths.

▶ Unrecognised deaths – for example, disenfranchised grief with gay people or those in unrecognised relationships.

▶ Multiple deaths – for example, major disasters.

▶ Preventable deaths – for example, those caused by drunk driving or medical negligence.

▶ Not knowing whether someone really has died – for example, wartime losses.

▶ Not being able to see the deceased.

▶ People going missing.

These situations are in themselves complicating factors for people having to deal with them. They tend to add to the stresses and strains of grief, and sometimes cause great anguish on top of the pain of losing a loved one. People in these situations often value opportunities to talk in depth about their feelings with trained counsellors simply because of the sheer volume and complexity of the issues they have been forced to handle.

It is also worth noting that, if people have been in a very close relationship with someone over many years, and have perhaps become very dependent upon them, then the implications of losing that person through death are particularly fraught with difficulty. It will feel as if their whole world has been destroyed. These are some of what we may call 'complicating factors' which make the grieving process for some people even harder to bear.

What can we do to help?

This is a deceptively easy question to ask, and perhaps a surprisingly difficult one to answer. So much of what we have talked about already in this manual has emphasised the individual nature of each person's journey through grief. It follows, therefore, that people will need different things from different people, and it is extraordinarily difficult to generalise.

To illustrate this point, we need do little more than list some of the different relationships people may have had to the deceased which will affect to a considerable degree how they respond and how they might seek to help someone who is a:

▶ manager at work

▶ colleague at work

▶ close friend

▶ casual acquaintance

▶ next-door neighbour

▶ close relative

▶ partner

▶ parent.

Not only will this relationship affect the sort of help you are able to offer, it will also determine what the person who is bereaved may be likely to expect. The manager will be expected to know the organisation's policy for compassionate leave, for example, and make this easily available. It is unlikely however that the manager will play the same role as a close friend who might take the bereaved person out for a meal or down to the pub for a drink.

One common strand, however, which should run through the responses of all of those involved is an understanding of what impact grief and loss can have upon people in their personal and professional lives. Courses such as the ones you are planning to run in your organisation or across a range of organisations will be of immense value in raising people's knowledge and awareness of these issues.

Such courses will also help people avoid some common pitfalls into which well-meaning friends and colleagues can sometimes fall. These include:

▶ telling or expecting people to 'snap out of it'

▶ telling people who have sustained a loss that there are 'plenty more fish in the sea'

▶ assuming that religious responses will be helpful for people who do not belong to faith communities

▶ avoiding people who have been bereaved because you feel uncomfortable and 'don't know what to say'

▶ being unwilling to listen when people want to talk about their loss.

Admittedly it can be difficult knowing what to say, but simply to acknowledge this can often be more supportive than avoiding the person altogether or coming out with a trite platitude.

There are organisations that offer help and support to people who have sustained serious losses, and we list some of these in Part Three. Some are somewhat loosely called 'self-help groups' or 'support groups'. It will be different in various parts of the country, and so it might be an idea for you to put some feelers out in your area to see what is available. Basically, self-help groups are opportunities for people who have had similar experiences to meet together on an occasional or regular basis to listen to each other, perhaps do things together, and so encourage each other on their respective painful journeys through grief. Such groups can literally be a 'godsend' to some, and positively the last thing on earth that others would want.

Many people find that the groups and organisations to which they already belong can be tremendously supportive in their time of loss. Pubs and clubs often foster a strong community spirit; faith communities frequently excel in offering friendship and practical care to people in need; special interest groups can be invaluable in helping people find a way forward. But not everyone is gregarious – many prefer to journey in relative solitude and would find enforced camaraderie counterproductive.

Other types of groups have a semi-professional or professional feel to them. These are organisations that have been set up specifically to help and support people who have experienced profound loss, and who perhaps are finding it particularly difficult to cope. Some of these are counselling organisations; some also offer a social dimension for bereaved people. Some have been set up specifically for people who have sustained a particular type of loss. Again, we have listed some examples in the final section of this manual, but we do not claim this to be exhaustive. It is worthwhile finding out what your particular area has to offer, and then to produce your own supplementary leaflet relevant for your course members.

It is also worth remembering that social workers also have a role to play, particularly if there are issues around disability, a person's inability to look after themselves or general vulnerability. They, together with the local Citizens' Advice Bureau, will be able to advise on a wide range of benefits for which people who have sustained a serious loss may be eligible.

To close this part, we invite you to reflect for a few moments on what sort of help and support you would appreciate in the event of a profound loss in your life, and what sort of help and support you definitely would not appreciate. It is worth jotting them down, not least because this will alert you to the sort of person you are, and how you might respond to great loss. (You may already know, of course, if this is familiar territory to you.) There is no guarantee whatsoever that anyone else will have an identical list to yours – and that is the point – just as you would wish to be treated as the unique individual which you undoubtedly are, so all the members who attend your training courses will feel the same way about themselves.

The secret – if there is one – for helping people through such difficult and painful times, is to treat them with the same respect and dignity as you yourself would wish to be treated in similar circumstances.

You and your workplace

So far we have focused on a lot of general issues which we feel confident will help you explore and understand some of the main themes around loss and grief. The final part of this background section explores briefly some of the workplace issues you will have to consider. Inevitably we cannot cover every aspect; there will be some issues pertinent to your own workplace that you will need to investigate and include in your training courses which we could not cover here without turning this manual into a less user-friendly encyclopaedia.

A good place to start is to obtain a copy of your organisation's staff care or workplace well-being policy and see what it has to say about how people who experience grief and loss will be treated by your organisation. Admittedly, such policies may be unfamiliar territory to some, so it is worth pausing for a moment to reflect on what this idea means. As Thompson (2015) explains:

> *'Staff care is a relatively new idea in management and organisational psychology literature. It refers to an approach to human resources based on the principle that the effectiveness of an organisation depends to a large extent on its staff being adequately supported in carrying out their duties. The major implication of this approach is that organisations should invest time, effort and money in providing sufficient and appropriate support for their staff.'*
> (pp89-90)

It may be, of course, that the policy does not mention this specifically. It may even be that your organisation does not have a staff care or workplace well-being policy at all. In which case, can you obtain a copy from a similar organisation to see how these issues are tackled?

You could make a checklist of some key issues to see how your organisation handles them – for example:

▶ Are there guidelines for compassionate leave?

▶ What is an employee who has been bereaved entitled to expect?

▶ Are there arrangements for an employee to be able to take unpaid leave without losing basic rights?

▶ Does the organisation allow flexi-working to help people experiencing grief and loss return to their employment?

▶ Health and safety: does the organisation recognise that people experiencing the stress of loss and grief may have reduced capacity to operate machinery and equipment safely?

▶ If there are major critical incidents in your organisation, how would employees be cared for effectively to help avoid the disabling symptoms of post-traumatic stress?

▶ Does your organisation have a confidential counselling service or 'employee assistance programme'?

This short list of questions to explore will immediately raise awareness of the extent to which your organisation both recognises and seeks to respond effectively to such issues.

It may be, however, that you discover little or no evidence of your organisation recognising such issues, let alone addressing them. It may be, for example, that the organisation has asked you to put on such training events precisely because the organisation recognises its deficits and wants you to help them do something about it.

It is probably more common that we think to find organisations that do not take these issues seriously enough, or even ignore them altogether. Organisational denial certainly exists, and it is not difficult to suggest some possible reasons. These might include:

▶ In the cut and thrust of highly competitive market places, there is no spare time to attend to such 'luxuries'.

▶ Such issues are private and individual, and should be dealt with in the employee's own time and at the employee's own expense.

▶ This is a tough world, and we expect our employees to be tough enough to cope and get on with the job.

▶ We don't want 'weak, namby-pamby' people in our workforce.

There are some important exercises to help you explore these issues further in Part Two of this manual.

Another key dimension to this issue is the role that trade unions and professional associations can and do play in this area. Their role has a particular emphasis on negotiating the best possible deals for the workforce within the wider economic constraints of the marketplace and economic prosperity of the organisation. It is well worth setting up an exploratory meeting with the trade union or professional association representatives or their equivalent, to see to what extent they are aware of the impact of the issues of grief and loss upon their members, and how they feel their organisation could improve its practice and its duty of care. Why not invite them to share in one of the training events with you to explore these issues?

Another difficult area concerns how your organisation deals with serious injury, major health problems (for example, heart attacks, strokes and so on) and deaths in the workplace:

▶ Who has responsibility for informing next of kin? How is this done and by whom?

▶ How are arrangements made for personal belongings to be collected?

▶ What care and support is offered to the immediate colleagues in the workplace?

▶ Does the organisation exercise any responsibility towards the family in helping them with some of the practical implications, such as life insurance claims and so on, and benefits resulting from the deceased's employment?

These are difficult issues, and many organisations would say (doubtless with fingers firmly crossed) that 'this has never happened to us'. But it might – and the moment when it does happen is precisely not the time to be wondering what the policy and practice is for dealing with it. These will be issues for management colleagues to work out, in consultation with trades unions and other appropriate human resources personnel.

One further advance has been the development of Common Core principles for health and social care workers working with adults at the end of life. These were prepared by Skills for Care and Skills for Health in partnership with the Department of Health[1].

At first glance you may think that this is relevant only to very old people reaching the end of their lives. But, on further reflection, it is clear that these issues can have a major impact upon a much wider section of the community. Many people currently in work will also have caring responsibilities for members of their family who are terminally ill.

However, many of you may well be working in the care sector and have to deal with these issues as part of your job. You will therefore be familiar with the role of Skills for Care, which forms a strategic overview of workforce needs in adult social care. This accounts for nearly 1.4 million workers, or five percent of England's workforce, spread over more than 38,000 employers. Skills for Care members are drawn from groups representing public, private and voluntary sector care employers, along with representatives of staff, trainers, service users and informal carers. Social care includes residential care, domiciliary care and social work with all its specialisms.

---

1 www.skillsforcare.org.uk/Documents/Topics/End-of-life-care/Common-core-principles-and-competences-for-social-care-and-health-workers-working-with-adults-at-the-end-of-life.pdf

The document sets out four key competences for staff working with people at the end of their lives including communication skills, assessment and care planning, advance care planning, symptom management, and maintaining comfort and well-being. The competences are underpinned by seven principles to drive workforce development irrespective of a worker's level of practice, occupational group or work setting. The competence document will help service managers develop services and practices; education and training providers with curriculum design and delivery; supervisors to effectively supervise staff, and frontline workers can use it as a reference when working with someone who is nearing the end of their life.

'There is no doubt that end of life care is one of the most difficult and emotional tasks that adult social care workers have to face and this easy-to-use guide is designed to support them and the people they work with through that process', says Skills for Care CEO, Andrea Rowe.

This section has attempted to raise some of the organisational issues that need to be explored if your organisation is to be a responsible employer, and to exercise an appropriate duty of care towards its employees. This manual will help you begin to explore these issues, but you will find in some areas that you need to seek more detailed guidance and help, especially with your legal obligations.

Part Two: Training and development

Introduction

This section contains a selection of training materials that have been designed to enable you to lead groups on the topic of grief and loss. Some seem deceptively straightforward, but there is always a chance that some group members will find some of the exercises challenging, moving, or perhaps a little upsetting if their own memories and feelings around loss are stimulated.

For this reason we suggest that for all sessions, however short or long in duration, you agree some basic ground rules so that everyone feels reasonably comfortable with what is being done. We also offer some 'icebreakers' or 'starters', which are designed to help the group begin to 'gel' – it is important that people working on such topics as grief and loss are able to develop a sense of belonging and trust in the group, and are not thrown in at the deep end.

The main exercises are grouped under topics, which you will find described and summarised below. This will help you select the exercises and materials that will best suit the needs of your training event.

Finally, we suggest some activities to bring the session to a close. We recommend that, for each session you use a 'starter' and a 'closer'. What takes place in between the two is obviously up to you to decide, depending upon the aims and objectives of your training session, the needs of the participants and the circumstances in which you are providing the training.

NB Please feel free to modify and adapt these exercises as you see fit so that they are most likely to meet your needs. They are not intended to be seen as set in stone. It is also always worth spending some time imaginatively working through how you will introduce and use each of these exercises so that you feel as comfortable about using them as you reasonably can. Please remember that unless you feel comfortable, the group members probably won't either. If you are reasonably confident about the materials you are introducing, the group members are much more likely to gain the benefit from them. If you are not an experienced trainer or tutor, don't hesitate to discuss the issues and any concerns you may have with a more experienced colleague or two.

Exercises overview

1. Welcome

This introductory exercise has been included to help put people at their ease. It is often the case that the first few minutes of a training event can be somewhat tense and uncertain, especially if people do not know each other. This exercise helps people to relax so that they can then get the best out of the rest of the session. It is intended to be light hearted and non-threatening.

2. Ground rules

This introductory exercise is designed to help you get the training event off to a good start by helping people to agree the ground rules which need to be observed if the session is to run smoothly and everyone in the group is to be treated with respect and courtesy.

3. Great expectations

You may believe that your group members think they know why they have come on your training event, but they may not! They may not know what to expect. So this introductory exercise helps both you and them to gain a clearer picture of what to expect in the training event. This will help people relax and be more comfortable – few things are worse than being afraid that things may happen in a group which might cause upset or embarrassment.

4. Listing the losses

This is an important exercise to help group members begin to appreciate the wide ranging nature and impact of loss, which can include some relatively small, even trivial events as well as the major losses of bereavement and divorce. This exercise provides a gentle and unthreatening way into discussing loss and our reactions to it.

5. Wishful thinking!

We would all like to be treated in certain ways if we feel vulnerable, particularly if we have experienced a serious loss. This exercise helps us to understand more clearly how we would like to be treated by others, and what this can tell us about how we should treat other people.

6. Creating a poster

This is a fun exercise designed to allow participants to consider important, emotive issues in a safe way. It explores similar themes to Exercise 5 and so can be used as a follow up to that exercise or as a freestanding activity in its own right.

7. Trying to make sense of it all

This exercise introduces people to the various ways in which we might be able to understand what happens to us when we experience a serious loss. It explores some of the 'models' for understanding these painful experiences.

8. Out of the ordinary

This exercise builds on the previous one and introduces people to some further aspects of loss and bereavement which fall outside some people's experience perhaps – it is called 'disenfranchised grief' and looks at, among other things, issues of loss for gay people.

9. Where do I feature in all of this?

This exercise will help people develop their awareness of their own attitudes and feelings about grief and loss. It encourages self-awareness as an important basis for responding sensitively and appropriately to other people's experiences of grief.

10. The DOs and DON'Ts of helping

This exercise is designed to help people become more aware of what can be helpful, or unhelpful, when trying to support someone who has experienced loss.

11. Celebrating diversity

This exercise is designed to help people recognise and celebrate diversity in the ways in which people from varying cultural backgrounds deal with grief and loss.

12. My boss really cares

This activity explores the role of organisational culture in terms of how an organisation responds to the needs of its employees who experience loss and bereavement.

13. It's got nothing to do with us

This exercise is designed to help people explore some of the reasons why organisations often do not take issues of grief and loss seriously in the workplace.

14. The conspiracy of silence

An alternative to Exercise 13, this activity explores similar issues but from the starting point of the language we use to discuss death and dying.

15. Men are from Mars

This exercise will help people explore ways in which women and men might deal with issues of grief and loss in different ways. It explores the complex but nonetheless important topic of the influence of gender expectations on the experience of loss.

16. Leaving was hard... but coming back was even worse

This exercise will help people explore issues around returning to work after a time of bereavement or serious loss.

17. Oh my God!

This exercise will help people explore issues of religion and spirituality and their relationship to grief and loss.

A note on timing

Each exercise contains guidelines on timing. Please note, however, that these are necessarily approximate. This is because the actual time taken will depend on a number of variables, not least the following:

▶ the size of the group

▶ the confidence and experience level of the participants

▶ the make up of the group (how many talkative people you have in the group!)

▶ the style of the trainer

▶ the confidence and experience level of the trainer.

It is therefore recommended that you consider timings carefully in undertaking your planning for the training, and that you prepare yourself to be as flexible as you reasonably can be. Experienced trainers should have little difficulty in achieving this, but if you are an inexperienced trainer you may wish to seek the advice and support of a more experienced colleague.

NB. All the PowerPoint slides, worksheets and handouts can be downloaded from www.pavpub.com/learning-from-practice-resources.

Exercise 1: Welcome

Aim

The aim of this activity is to help people feel welcome and 'at home' in the group. It is intended as a light-hearted introductory session to put people at their ease and create a positive working environment.

Materials

No equipment is needed for this exercise.

Timing

This activity should take between 10 and 30 minutes (depending on which option you take) but could be longer if you have a large group. The time should be divided up roughly as follows:

Introduction: 3 to 5 minutes
Step 1:
(Options A to D): 5 to 15 minutes
(Option E): 10 to 20 minutes
Step 2: concluding comments: 10 to 20 minutes

Activity

▶ Introduce yourself and welcome the participants. Explain to the group that this introductory activity is a short 'icebreaker' designed to help create a relaxed atmosphere where people feel comfortable.

▶ **Step 1** – You will need to choose one of the following five options:

  ▶ **Option A:** Ask the participants to introduce themselves by name, and to say something about themselves which you couldn't tell by looking at them.

  ▶ **Option B:** Ask them to share a 'new and good' event – that is, something good that has happened to them during the past week.

  ▶ **Option C:** Ask them to say which famous person they would like to take out for a meal in a posh restaurant and why.

  ▶ **Option D:** Ask them to share one light-hearted, embarrassing moment.

  ▶ **Option E:** Ask them to work in pairs for five minutes and to discuss some of their 'outside of work' hobbies or interests. Then ask each pair to introduce each other to the main group and briefly summarise the points they discussed.

▶ Move round the group fairly quickly, and do not worry too much if someone gets tongue-tied – come back to them, if necessary, after the rest of the group has had their say. But do try to make sure, as far as possible, that everyone says something – it is harder for a participant to join in the longer they stay silent.

▶ **Step 2 –** To draw the exercise to a close make a few concluding comments with a lot of reassurance thrown in, and thank them for their input so far. Point out that they have all now spoken in the main group at least once and should now feel more confident about doing it a second time by joining in the discussions. You may now wish to make some comments about the rest of the course (give an overview of the content, for example).

Exercise 2: Ground rules

Aim

The aim of this activity is to ensure that everyone is comfortable with the style of training you are planning to use and the boundaries which need to be set. This is an important part of any training course, but it is particularly important in relation to a course that deals with such emotive topics as loss and grief.

Materials

A flip chart and marker pens

Blu Tack or masking tape

Slide 1: Some basic ground rules

Timing

This is variable. It could take between 25 and 45 minutes if you wish to do it thoroughly, but it is possible to reduce the discussion time and achieve a reasonably good result in 20 to 25 minutes if you have less time to devote to this process. The overall timing can be broken down as follows:

Introduction: 5 minutes

Groupwork: 10 to 20 minutes

Feedback and discussion: 5 to 10 minutes

Summary and conclusion: 5 minutes

Activity

▶ Remind participants about any 'housekeeping' arrangements – for example, fire exits, toilets, what to do if the fire alarm sounds, arrangements for refreshments, confirm finishing time, what arrangements for urgent messages for participants and so on.

▶ Check that everyone is happy to turn off all mobile phones. If this creates genuine problems for some, then you need to gain agreement that, as soon as it rings (or ideally vibrates) the group member immediately leaves the room to take the call.

▶ Ask the participants to get into groups of two or three, and for each group to come up with some suggestions for ground rules which they feel will be important for the success of this event. (If they look blank, you can suggest some examples, such as not interrupting others, or not falling asleep during the session!). After a few minutes, you can either:

  ▶ ask the pairs to link up with another group to swap notes and agree on a common set of ground rules to present to the whole group, which you can write up on the flip chart.

  ▶ ask each group to report back to you, so that you can write them on to the flip chart.

▶ When you have all the suggested ground rules on the flipchart, you need to ask the group whether they would all be happy to adopt them all, or whether some need to be removed or modified. The final list then becomes the ground rules agreement for your course and should be displayed through the session(s).

Notes

▶ It is worthwhile having your own list available, in case the groups get 'stuck' or forget something really basic. To help with this, you can use **Slide 1: Some basic ground rules** to present your ideas to the group. Points to consider including are:

  ▶ We expect everyone to participate as fully as they can.

  ▶ No one will be pressurised into saying or doing anything they do not feel comfortable with.

  ▶ We will not interrupt each other.

  ▶ No one should dominate the discussions.

  ▶ If you get upset, it is OK to sit quietly, or withdraw to another room for a short time.

  ▶ The contents of the discussions will remain confidential to the group members, and no one, including the trainer, will divulge anything to anyone who is not a member of the group.

  ▶ The trainer will keep to time and will end punctually. Group members will also seek to be punctual.

  ▶ Everyone is expected to contribute in some way or other, and to take responsibility for their own learning.

Add any other points you feel are important.

▶ This exercise can be completed fairly quickly if you feel time is at a premium, or it can be used to full effect by allocating up to three quarters of an hour to it.

▶ If group members seem to be 'flagging' it is important to move forward and achieve agreement. To be on the safe side, you might even like to have some of your suggestions ready prepared on a flip chart sheet in order to help group members make progress. It is better to do it relatively quickly rather than not at all, but the benefits of group working and developing trust and good communications from allocating 45 minutes to this exercise cannot be underestimated, as it is clearly important to establish acceptable ways of working together when tackling such emotive topics as loss and grief.

Exercise 3: Great expectations

Aim

To enable the trainer and group members clarify what they hope to get from the training event.

Materials

Flip chart and marker pens
Slide 2: Great expectations (optional)

Timing

This exercise is likely to take 20 to 30 minutes, divided up as follows:
Introduction: 2 to 3 minutes
Work in pairs: 5 minutes
Feedback and discussion: 5 to 20 minutes (depending on the size of the group)
Summary and conclusion: 5 to 20 minutes (depending on the size of the group)

Activity

▶ Begin by commenting that people come on such events for a whole variety of reasons – we hope that most members want to be there, although on occasion there are events which people have been mandated to attend. As a result, they could feel resentful and unwilling to participate freely. It is important that everybody is clear at the outset about what they hope to get out of the event.

▶ Then ask the participants to break into pairs and spend five minutes discussing the following two topics (using **Slide 2: Great expectations** if you wish):

  ▶ Why have I come into this training event?

  ▶ What am I hoping to get out of it?

▶ After five minutes (or slightly longer if you wish) reconvene the whole group and ask each pair to report their answers. List the main points on the flip chart under the two headings, using one column for each topic. If there are expectations which cannot be met, say so in a clear, unapologetic way. Everyone knows then what not to expect.

▶ Following this, briefly outline the topics and the timetable for the session. You might like to have prepared this in advance on a handout which can be distributed. Alternatively, you could put it on the flip chart or even prepare a presentation slide.

Exercise 4: Listing the losses

Aim

To help group members appreciate the wide-ranging nature and impact of loss.

Materials

Flip chart, paper and marker pens
Blu Tack or masking tape
Worksheet 1: Listing the losses

Have some sheets of flip chart paper ready – one sheet for each group of between three and five members, depending on the overall group size. However, it will work best if there are at least four groups, so the group size could be three if this is the only way to ensure four groups altogether.

Timing

This activity should take between 40 and 50 minutes, divided up roughly as follows:

Introduction: 5 minutes
Step 1: Groupwork: 10 minutes
Step 2: Working in pairs: 10 minutes
Step 3: Feedback and discussion: 15 to 20 minutes
Summary and conclusion: 5 minutes

Activity

▶ You need to explain that loss is a common experience for all of us. We tend to associate grief and loss particularly with death and bereavement, but in fact the experience of loss, and the impact it has upon us, is widespread. (You may wish to draw on the material in Part One of the manual to help you prepare for this introduction.)

▶ **Step 1 –** Ask participants to divide into small groups and give one sheet of flip chart paper and a marker pen to each group. Invite them to make as long a list as possible of all the losses they can think of, large or small. See how many they can think of. If they seem a bit stuck at the beginning, we suggest you use one or two of the losses listed in Part One or any others you may be able to think of that are particularly relevant to the staff group that you are working with.

▶ Move around the group and give help where necessary. Keep it quite light. When you feel the lists are fairly full, ask the groups to attach them to the walls, preferably one on each wall. If that is difficult keep them spaced as far apart as possible. Then invite everyone to move round the room reading the other groups' lists, and comment on what others have included, as well as perhaps what they have left off their lists. Allow about five minutes for this. This helps get the group to gel and mingle.

▶ **Step 2** – Invite participants to work in pairs, preferably with someone they do not know very well. Distribute copies of **Worksheet 1: Listing the losses**. Invite them each to think about an incident that they would be happy to talk about which involved loss of some sort. In pairs, ask them to tell each other briefly about the loss and why it was significant. When each of them has 'told their story', ask them to jot down on the worksheet what they can remember feeling about this particular loss.

▶ **Step 3** – Finally, attach all the worksheets to one of the walls where everyone can see them easily, and group everyone together. Invite the group to comment on the impact of seeing all these feelings being mentioned. Use this as the basis of a discussion of the significance of loss.

▶ Draw the exercise to a close by commenting on the range and perhaps the power of the feelings that have been mentioned. Loss is not an easy experience to deal with, even on a small scale, and our reactions are often jumbled together and difficult to sort out. Often they affect how we behave and how we deal with other people, at home and also at work.

Worksheet 1: Listing the losses

Choose a partner, ideally someone you do not know very well.

1. Think about an incident that you would be happy to talk about which involved some sort of loss in your life. Then tell each other briefly about the loss and why it was significant.

2. Now jot down the feelings which this loss caused you to experience. (**NB** You will be invited to display this worksheet on the notice board with all the others at the end of this section of the exercise.)

Exercise 5: Wishful thinking!

Aim

To help group members begin to understand and reflect upon how they would like to be treated, especially at work, if they had experienced a serious loss.

Materials

Flipchart paper and marker pen.

Worksheet 2: Codes of practice

You will need a convenient room to complete this exercise, with sufficient space for people to spread out.

Timing

Allow 60 to 80 minutes, depending on whether you use some or all of the material in this exercise. This should be broken down as follows:

Step 1: Introduction: 5 minutes

Work in pairs: 5 minutes

Feedback: 5 minutes

Step 2: Groupwork: 10 minutes

Feedback: 10 minutes

Step 3: Groupwork: 15 minutes

Step 4: Discussion and feedback: 15 to 25 minutes

Summary and conclusion: 5 minutes

Activity

▶ All being well, people should find this exercise fun, which is an important ingredient in training – so do enjoy it!

▶ Explain that, obviously, we all hope that we never have to deal with a major loss in our lives, but there is every chance that we will have to at some point. Someone close to us will die – maybe suddenly, maybe after a long illness.

▶ **Step 1** – Invite participants to get into pairs, preferably with someone that they have not previously worked with in the group. Explain that you would like them to spend the next five minutes discussing together how they would like to be treated at work if they experienced a serious loss in their lives.

▶ Give out copies of **Worksheet 2: Codes of practice**, which they can use to make notes. After five minutes or so, invite them to call out their responses which you can then write on the flip chart. Invite comments from the group when the list is complete. Feel free to add any further points of your own.

▶ **Step 2** – Ask them as a group if they know what the organisation's policy is about compassionate leave, for example. What are their rights? If they do not know, you might like to start a further chart on a wall, indicating issues that need to be explored, questions that need to be answered or information that needs to be discovered.

▶ You could then ask them to give examples from their own experience at work of how people experiencing loss really have been treated by management or by their fellow workers. No names should be used but encourage examples of both 'good practice' and 'bad practice'. If the group are not very forthcoming, they can provide answers and responses in a hypothetical way – that is:

   ▶ What do they imagine an unhelpful response might be?

   ▶ What might be the difficulties, or dangers even, of not recognising that someone is trying to cope with a serious loss?

▶ **Step 3** – Invite participants to move into small groups (three or four per group) and ask them to draw up a code of best practice for their organisation, detailing how they feel it should respond when someone at work has experienced a serious loss. Be realistic – the organisation's work still has to go on, but how important is it for there to be a culture of caring and awareness in the workplace?

▶ **Step 4** – Place the completed 'codes of practice' around the four walls, well spaced apart. Invite the group to move around and read and discuss the other groups' contributions. A lot of useful discussion is likely to take place 'on the hoof', so please don't feel that you have to draw people back into the plenary too quickly. Try to circulate, and note the key points arising from their discussions.

▶ Next, invite the group to reconvene, and ask them to try to identify why it is important for an organisation to recognise the importance of grief and loss in its workforce. Use this as the basis of a discussion to explore these important issues.

▶ Use the last few minutes to summarise the main learning points to have emerged from the discussion (or ask the group to do so).

Worksheet 2: Codes of practice

If you were to experience a major loss in your life, how would you want to be treated at work? What would you regard as a helpful response from your employers?

Exercise 6: Creating a poster

Aim

This is a fun activity that should allow participants to explore complex and emotive issues in a safe way. It involves designing a poster.

Materials

Flip chart paper and a large number of marker pens in different colours

Blu Tack or masking tape

Tables for laying out flip chart paper or a floor covering suitable for people to work on the floor.

Timing

This activity should take approximately 50 minutes, divided up as follows:

Introduction: 5 minutes

Step 1: Groupwork: 15 minutes

Step 2: Display of artwork: 5 minutes

Step 3: Feedback and discussion: 20 minutes

Summary and conclusion: 5 minutes

Activity

▶ Begin by explaining to the group that this is a light-hearted exercise that involves giving them the opportunity to create a poster in small groups. Reassure them straight away that they do not need to have any drawing skills to make this an effective learning experience.

▶ **Step 1 –** Invite the participants to form small groups and ask each group to produce a poster for their organisation, illustrating the importance of dealing sensitively with issues of grief and loss in the workplace. Tell them that you are not looking for any 'right answers', but rather giving them the opportunity to be creative so that, later in the exercise, there can be a discussion of what can be learned about grief and loss by considering the issues that arise. Please stress again that this is a fun exercise where no artistic talent whatsoever is needed – everyone should 'have a go' at creating this poster! Each group will need one poster-sized sheet of paper and some variously coloured marker pens.

NB Some groups may work much faster than others. If a group finishes ahead of schedule, invite them to think about whether their poster tells us anything about: (i) how grief is seen in the workplace; and (ii) how it should be seen.

▶ **Step 2** – Once the groups are ready, display the posters around the walls and express appreciation for their creative hard work. Invite the participants to circulate and have a look at what their colleagues in other groups have come up with.

▶ **Step 3** – Reconvene the main group and ask them whether they have anything they want to ask of the other groups – for example, why they chose their particular approach. Use this as a lead-in to a discussion of loss and grief in the work place, concentrating on (i) how they feel grief is seen in the workplace; and (ii) how they feel it should be seen.

▶ It will probably be useful to introduce into the discussion the notion of a 'conspiracy of silence' – that is, the idea that people often feel uncomfortable about discussing these issues and will therefore tend to ignore them.

▶ There is no need to undertake a critical appraisal of the artwork, but it may be worth exploring the question of whether there is anything significant about the approaches taken by the different groups (the symbolism they use, the language they draw upon and so on). This can be a useful vein of discussion material to explore.

▶ Use the last few minutes to summarise the main learning points from the exercise (or ask the group to do so).

Exercise 7: Trying to make sense of it all

Aim

To introduce people to some of the ways in which attempts have been made to 'make sense' of grief.

Materials

Flip chart, paper and marker pens
Slide 2: Great expectations
Slide 3: The Dual Process Approach
Slide 4: The idea of stages
Slide 5: The tasks of grief
Worksheet 3: Trying to make sense of it all
Handout 1: Approach 1: The Dual Process Model
Handout 2: Approach 2: The idea of stages
Handout 3: Approach 3: The tasks of grief
Handout 4: Approach 4: Finding new meanings

Timing

This is a substantial session which could require between two hours and two hours 40 minutes to complete. However, it could be modified to take less, depending upon how detailed a discussion you wish people to undertake. It is important to do justice to these themes, however, and to allow time for this.

If you do choose to undertake the session in full, you will need to consider also allowing time for a break in the middle, as expecting over two hours of concentration without a break is very demanding.

The specific timings should be as follows:

Step 1: Introduction and presentation: 20 to 30 minutes

Steps 2 to 5: Groupwork: 20 to 25 minutes per topic (total of between 1hr 20 and 1hr 40) minutes

Step 6: Feedback and discussion: 15 to 25 minutes

Summary and conclusion: 5 to 10 minutes

Activity

▶ Begin by explaining to the participants that this activity is geared towards helping them to develop their understanding of how different people have tried to make sense of the complex world of bereavement, loss and grief. Emphasise that it is not intended to turn them into experts on the subject, but rather to give them the opportunity to consider different approaches to the subject so that they can approach in a better-informed way the difficult task of helping people cope with loss and grief.

▶ There needs to be a presentation to introduce this session, based upon the set of presentation slides (Slides 2 to 5), which accompany this exercise. The presentation need not be a lengthy or detailed one, as the purpose is to give people a brief overview of how some of the leading practitioners and writers in the field of grief and loss have tried to help us to understand, and possibly even make sense of, this range of experiences.

▶ You may of course like to draw on some of the material in the appendix of this manual to add to your presentation, which in any case you are strongly encouraged to read as part of your own preparation. We suggest that you issue copies of **Worksheet 3: Trying to make sense of it all** to help note taking.

▶ **Step 1** – Presentation. Themes covered:

  ▶ The Dual Process Approach

  ▶ The idea of stages

  ▶ The tasks of grief

  ▶ Finding new meanings

▶ **Step 2** – Divide the main group into four subgroups. Give each group one of the approaches or themes to discuss, using the accompanying **Handouts 1 to 4**. Each group will be asked to consider how helpful or otherwise each approach or theme is, based on their experience and that of people they know who have experienced serious loss (keep in touch with each group in case they need help or support).

▶ **Steps 3 to 5** – For Step 3, repeat Step 2, but this time issue each subgroup with a different approach. Repeat this again for Steps 4 and 5. Each of the approaches or themes will have been circulated to each group so that, by the end of Step 5, each group will have discussed each of these approaches or themes.

▶ **Step 6** – Plenary discussion. Invite each group in turn to introduce their response to one of the approaches or themes and allow the other groups the opportunity to add their comments. In this way you should be able to ensure that the whole group obtains an overview of the material covered relating to the four approaches.

▶ Write up the main points about each approach or theme on a separate sheet of flip chart paper.

▶ Finally, invite a discussion about which approaches or themes seem to the group to be most helpful. As a closing statement, please remind people that everyone is different and that there are not necessarily right or wrong ways of dealing with these painful topics.

▶ Go round the group asking each person to say briefly one thing which they have gained from this session that has proved interesting and helpful.

Worksheet 3: Trying to make sense of it all

Dual Process Approach

The idea of stages

The tasks of grief

Finding new meanings

Worksheet 3: Trying to make sense of it all

Exercise 8: Out of the ordinary!

Aim

To introduce group members to aspects of bereavement that are often beyond or outside the experience or understanding of the majority of people, but which are important for us to explore. The formal name is 'disenfranchised grief'.

Materials

Flip chart
Paper and marker pens
Worksheet 4: Out of the ordinary (1)
Worksheet 5: Out of the ordinary (2)
Slide 7: Disenfranchised grief
A4 plain paper

Timing

This exercise could last for between 1 hour 30 minutes and 1 hour 40 minutes depending on the size of your group. It is therefore worthwhile seeing whether you wish to use all or just some of the materials offered here as part of your overall programme. The overall timing should be broken down roughly as follows:

Introduction and Step 1: 10 to 15 minutes
Steps 2 and 3: Groupwork 1: 20 to 25 minutes
Step 4: Feedback 1: 10 minutes
Step 5: Groupwork 2: 30 minutes
Step 6: Feedback 2: 15 minutes
Summary and conclusion: 5 minutes

Activity

▶ One of our earlier exercises helped us explore the wide range of losses which can happen in our lives. Bereavement is one of the most painful experiences on this wide spectrum of losses. Within bereavement itself, however, there are also many varied experiences – some of these are easily recognisable and might be said to have 'public approval'.

▶ There are other types of bereavement, however, where it is almost impossible to acknowledge that you are going through a period of grief – if you did, you might attract serious disapproval. It is important for us to be aware that people going through such experiences will almost have an 'extra layer' to their grief, which could make it even harder to bear.

▶ **Step 1** – Using the flip chart, invite the whole group to call out some of the situations where this type of private grief could be experienced. List their responses on the flip chart. Alternatively, ask the participants to work in pairs to produce their lists and then go round the pairs asking for their responses.

▶ At this stage, simply record their responses, although you may need from time to time to clarify them.

▶ **Step 2** – Exploring the definition. Display **Slide 7: Disenfranchised grief** to help people understand exactly what we mean generally by disenfranchised grief.

▶ Definition: Disenfranchised grief refers to grief that is experienced when a loss cannot be openly acknowledged, socially sanctioned or publicly mourned. There is no perceived 'right to grieve' (Doka, 1989).

▶ Invite the group to ask any questions about this definition in order to clarify the meaning. It is important that they have a clear understanding of the term before proceeding to Step 3.

▶ **Step 3** – Depending upon the number of examples you have identified in the previous step (do use the material provided in Part One of the manual on disenfranchised grief as your own checklist in case they need prompting), divide the group into an equivalent number of subgroups so that they can work on one topic per group.

▶ Invite each group to choose a topic (you may need to offer some guidance to make sure that all topics are allocated). Reassure people that no prior knowledge is needed for this exercise.

▶ Using **Worksheet 4: Out of the ordinary (1)**, invite each group to discuss the following topics:

1. What are the factors that make this an example of disenfranchised grief?

2. What might be the fears and worries of someone experiencing this kind of loss?

3. What sort of help and support might be helpful?

▶ **Step 4** – Invite feedback from each group. List their responses on a separate sheet for each question so that you build up a common list of comments and responses for each question.

▶ **Step 5** – Divide the main group into subgroups of four or five members per group. Their task is to prepare a leaflet to be generally available to people, explaining what this type of loss is and offering some guidance and suggested help and support. Distribute copies of **Worksheet 5: Out of the ordinary (2)**. The leaflet should be A4 size, with a layout as each group prefers.

▶ **Step 6** – Leaflet exchange and feedback. Pass the leaflets round and invite comments – it doesn't matter if they are incomplete. Is there any chance that some of these ideas could be used by participants to produce a leaflet design and proposal for their organisation(s)?

► **Conclusion.** Go round the group asking each group member to identify one benefit which they have gained from the session.

Note on timings

As we said at the outset, you need to decide whether you are going to use all or just some of the material we have provided in this exercise. The timings are approximate, of course, and will depend upon how many members you have in your group. Generally speaking, however, if a group is going well it is worth being generous in your time allocation. These exercises have been devised in such a way, however, that if the group seems to be flagging, there is something else you can move on to easily to explore the topic further.

Worksheet 4: Out of the ordinary (1)

Choose an example of disenfranchised grief. In your group, please discuss and make notes on the following topics:

1. What are the factors that make this an example of disenfranchised grief?

2. What might be the fears and worries of someone experiencing this kind of loss?

3. What sort of help and support might be helpful to someone experiencing this kind of loss?

Worksheet 5: Out of the ordinary (2)

Your task is to devise an information leaflet about disenfranchised grief which can be made generally available in your workplace. It will need to offer some explanations of what this term means and offer some guidance and suggested help and support.

Size A4 – but you choose whether it is to be a folded leaflet or not.

To get you started: what alternative name for disenfranchised grief will you use as a title heading for the leaflet which will grab people's attention?

Exercise 9: Where do I feature in all this?

Aim

To help group members develop their awareness of their own feelings, and perhaps even 'hang-ups', about grief and loss.

Materials

Worksheet 6: Where do I feature in all this?

Timing

This activity will take between 60 and 80 minutes, divided up as follows:

Introduction: (Step 1) 5 minutes
Individual work: (Step 2) 5 minutes
Groupwork: (Step 3) 30 to 35 minutes
Feedback and discussion: (Step 4) 20 to 30 minutes
Summary and conclusion: 5 minutes

Activity

▶ This is an important exercise that has the potential to run and run, or very quickly to run out of steam. Why? Because it is quite a sensitive area and group members may either warm to it and welcome it or find it too uncomfortable. It is important in your planning, therefore, to come to some preliminary judgement about how you think the group will respond. You may not know, of course, but it is important to reflect on this for a while nevertheless.

▶ The exercise invites your group members to reflect on and discuss a series of questions in small groups, beginning with some individual worksheets to get them into the subject. It is important, therefore, to remind them of the 'ground rules' – no one is expected to discuss anything they are not comfortable with. But try to keep this reminder as light as possible: you do not want to be giving a 'heavy' message at the outset that contradicts the purpose of the session. It is worth reminding people to be sensitive towards each other and that if someone gets a bit upset, it is OK to remain quiet in the group or to move to a neutral space in the room for a while.

▶ **Step 1** – Introduce the exercise by explaining that it is often helpful for all of us to look at ourselves from time to time to see how we cope with loss, and whether there are particular difficulties we encounter. If there are, this should not be surprising because, by definition, loss is (or certainly can be) painful, distressing, and can put us 'off balance' for a while. Explain that this is a session where we can begin to explore this sort of issue in a safe and supportive setting, at the pace and level which we find comfortable. There is no right or wrong way of exploring these issues; all we need to do is to listen to our own feelings and opinions and to those of others in a gentle, respectful way.

▶ **Step 2 –** Invite people to get into groups of three, with people they feel comfortable to share this sort of discussion with. Use the full space of the room (or rooms) so that each group has 'its own space' as far as possible. Distribute copies of **Worksheet 6: Where do I feature in all this?** and ask people to spend a few minutes quietly reflecting on the topics raised and jotting down their responses to them if they wish to.

▶ **Step 3 –** Invite the groups to begin to share their responses to the various questions and topics on the worksheet. It may be easiest to take them in turn, but this is not necessary. Your role is to be outside the discussions but to be aware if any groups get stuck, and to help them move forward to the next issue. Be particularly aware if someone seems to be getting upset. If someone needs time out, that is OK – they can perhaps sit quietly in the group or move to a neutral space in the room.

▶ **Step 4 –** Bring them together into one group. State clearly that the material they have been discussing in their small groups is confidential to those groups, and that the closing session will be brief and is intended just to highlight people's reactions to the exercise. Invite them, as they feel ready, to identify:

  ▶ something they have learned

  ▶ something they will try to do differently as a result of this exercise.

▶ At this stage you might like to mention that there are various agencies which can offer specialist help and support for people who wish to explore their feelings and opinions around grief and loss in greater depth. You may wish to have a leaflet on such organisations available, based on parts of our own reference section in the appendix of this manual (p103).

▶ And, finally, ask everyone to mention briefly something they are looking forward to in the next day or two. As people leave – or have a break – be aware in case anyone seems a little upset or withdrawn and might appreciate a word from you.

Note

The final aspect of the exercise in the plenary is important to help people acknowledge what they have gained from it for themselves, and also to give them a future focus of something they will enjoy in the immediate future. This helps them to leave the session in a positive frame of mind.

Worksheet 6: Where do I feature in all this?

1. Spend a few moments thinking about a 'medium to fairly large size' loss which you have experienced in your life – nothing that was so traumatic that you will get too upset talking about it, but something that had an impact on you. What were the feelings you experienced?

2. In your groups of three, spend some time telling each other briefly about the loss event and your reactions to it.

3. Move on then to explore what, if anything, helped you cope with the loss. Were there things which made it more difficult to cope? How did other people react to you and treat you?

4. What are the main things you have learned from this experience? What might you do differently next time?

Exercise 10: The DOs and DON'Ts of helping

Aim

To help group members become more aware of what can be helpful or unhelpful when trying to support someone who has experienced loss.

Materials

Flip chart paper and marker pens
Worksheet 7: Responding to loss

Timing

This exercise is likely to take 30 to 40 minutes, broken down roughly as follows:

Introduction: 3 to 5 minutes
Groupwork: (Step 1) 15 minutes
Feedback and discussion: (Step 2) 10 to 15 minutes
Summary and conclusion: (Step 3) 5 minutes

Activity

▶ This is a relatively short exercise that can be used to round off a session. It is intended to be an essentially practical activity, and not too 'heavy'. But it is important to focus on some of the main issues of what it means to help.

▶ **Step 1** – Divide the participants into small groups of three or four, with two sheets of flip chart paper and a few marker pens. Ask them to mark one sheet of paper with the title DOs, and the second sheet with the title DON'Ts. Allow about 15 minutes for the participants to put down onto each sheet of paper as many suggestions as they can think of as to how they might help someone experiencing loss.

▶ **Step 2** – Call the group together and put all the DOs on one wall, and all the DONTs on another wall. Distribute copies of **Worksheet 7: Responding to loss** and explain that this can be used to make guidance notes for future reference based on the learning gained from this activity.

▶ Invite some general discussion on the completed lists and use this as the basis for a discussion about the complexities of responding to loss and the need to handle such situations carefully and sensitively. End by saying that these can only be guidelines, but they are worth thinking about for us as individuals and how we respond to people who experience loss.

▶ **Step 3** – Use the last few minutes to sum up the main learning points that have emerged (or ask the group to do so).

Worksheet 7: Responding to loss

DOs

DON'Ts

Exercise 11: Celebrating diversity

Aim

To help group members both to recognise and also to celebrate diversity in the ways in which people from varying cultural backgrounds deal with grief and loss.

Materials

Flip chart and marker pens

Newspaper or magazine pictures illustrating different ways in which people show their grief (optional)

Timing

This is a substantial activity that can take up to two and a quarter hours. The session can be broken down roughly as follows:

Introduction: 5 to 10 minutes

Groupwork 1: (Step 1) 20 minutes

Feedback and discussion: (Step 2) 30 to 40 minutes

Summary and conclusion: (Step 3) 5 minutes

Optional extra 1: 30 minutes

Optional extra 2: 20 to 30 minutes

Activity

▶ To state that we live in a multicultural society is, in itself, an unremarkable observation. There is a wide variety in how people approach the issues and rituals surrounding death, dying and bereavement in particular, depending upon their cultural identity and whether or not they belong to a faith community. This session is intended to do no more than introduce people to these issues and to increase awareness of their importance in this area of human experience. The benchmark of a successful outcome will not be your ability as trainer to answer all their questions about cultural diversity or the variety of rituals used by faith communities – that would be wholly unrealistic. Success may be measured instead by the amount of interest shown in the subject and the willingness of group members to go and find out further information for themselves.

▶ For this reason, we suggest at the end a project which you might like to consider as a group as a follow up to this session (optional extra 2).

▶ One further point deserves mention. Very often sessions like these can start off from a mistaken assumption that 'difference' is something which marks out other people. So, an all-white group, for example, might assume that this session is only about black or Asian people. This would be to miss the point. The starting point for your group will be the conviction that we all have some different and perhaps contrasting experiences from our various backgrounds, especially when it comes to considering the issues of death and dying and bereavement. So the session will begin from the experiences of your group members, which they can 'own' and, we hope, also celebrate. From that starting point we can then move on to a wider appreciation of diversity. You should therefore consider carefully how best to put these ideas across in a short introduction to this activity.

▶ **Step 1** – Invite participants to move into small groups of between four and six people. Their task is to discuss together how their attitudes and customs around death and dying and bereavement are similar to or different from their parents' and their grandparents' generations.

▶ **Step 2** – Plenary discussion. Make lists of the sort of things which are different between these generations. This will give you a good springboard to identify some of the cultural differences within your group. It is likely that these will emerge naturally as the discussion unfolds. What about cultural groups and communities who are not represented within your group's experience? What do we know about their attitudes and rituals around death, dying and bereavement?

▶ **Step 3** – Use the last few minutes to summarise the main learning points to have emerged (or ask the group to do so). If you are using either of the optional extras below, you will need to postpone this summary and conclusion until after that.

▶ **Optional extra 1** – If you have brought pictures, newspaper cuttings and so on which illustrate different cultural perspectives (or if group members were asked to bring them in advance), these can be displayed on the walls and discussion invited about the issues they are illustrating. Are there representatives from these groups and communities in your workplace whose needs we should be aware of in case of bereavement and loss? What, if anything, should your organisation be doing to increase awareness of these issues?

▶ **Optional extra 2** – Follow-up project. If particular issues have arisen concerning the needs of cultural and religious groups in your area or workplace, you may wish to create a follow-up project, whereby group members undertake to find out and perhaps present their findings to a later session or to produce an information pack.

Exercise 12: My boss really cares

Aim

To explore the role of organisational culture in terms of how it responds to the needs of its employees who experience loss and bereavement.

Materials

Flip chart paper and marker pens.

Copies of an organisation's policy on staff care, staff support or workplace well-being (there should be enough copies to ensure that every group member has one).

Slide 8: Staff care (optional)

Handout 5: My boss really cares

Timing

This is another major exercise that can last between 1 hour and 5 minutes and 2 hours and 40 minutes. It can be broken down roughly as follows:

Introduction: 10 to 15 minutes

Groupwork 1: (Step 1) 30 to 45 minutes

Groupwork 2: (Step 2) 20 to 25 minutes

Feedback and discussion: (Step 3) 30 to 40 minutes

Summary and conclusion: (Step 4) 5 minutes

Optional extra: 30 minutes

Activity

▶ This exercise requires a certain level of preparation on your part as the trainer. You need to obtain a copy of a staff care policy (or similar such policy or policies) and to become familiar with it. If you work for an organisation which has such a policy, you will be able to use that one. In the event of your having to find one from another organisation, you may have to do some networking to find one which is user-friendly for your purposes. To save time in the group session, you need to identify some key issues to check out against the policy. See the list in **Handout 5: My boss really cares.** You may wish to use **Slide 8: Staff care** to display these for the group.

▶ Begin by introducing the concept of the organisation's responsibility to exercise a duty of care towards its employees (for example, under health and safety legislation), and that this is enshrined in the staff care policy (or its equivalent). In the event of your organisation no having such a policy, you will need to explain this and introduce an alternative policy you have obtained from another organisation. The exercise is very similar in either case.

▶ **Step 1** – Divide the group into subgroups of two or three in each. Distribute copies of the handout. When they are settled into these groups, explain that the purpose of the exercise is to look at the policy document in small groups and to identify first what the policy has to say about each of the headings suggested on the handout. Also ask them to see if any other issues are identified in the policy.

NB. If the document is substantial, you may wish to give them some page or paragraph numbers to save time (or provide them with an edited version of the policy).

▶ Each group should be asked to make a note of the key elements of the policy as it affects the care for employees who have been bereaved or who have sustained serious loss.

▶ **Step 2** – Invite each group to reflect upon what they have discovered by joining forces with another group to share findings. The next step is for each of these larger groups:

   ▶ First, to evaluate the policy and how effective they think it is.

   ▶ Second, to identify any issues that have not been included in the policy. These should be noted on a flip chart.

▶ **Step 3** – Each group should be asked to report back to the plenary, identifying:

   ▶ their evaluation of the policy as it stands

   ▶ any omissions from the policy.

▶ Next, convene a plenary discussion to seek some agreement on how the policy should be improved.

NB. Organisations that do not have a policy would need to conclude the session by seeking to draft a policy for consideration by management, or if it is a group of managers, for consideration by the unions and employees (allow an additional 30 minutes).

▶ **Step 4** – Use the last few minutes to summarise the main learning points to have emerged (or ask the group to do so).

Exercise 13: It's got nothing to do with us

Aim

To explore reasons why organisations often do not take issues of grief and loss seriously in the workplace.

Materials

Flip chart paper and marker pens
Blu Tack or masking tape
Worksheet 8: It's got nothing to do with us

Timing

This activity is likely to take about an hour and three quarters, broken down roughly as follows:

Introduction: 5 minutes
Groupwork: (Step 1) 15 minutes
Feedback: (Step 2) 10 minutes
Groupwork: (Step 3) 30 minutes
Feedback and discussion: (Step 4) 30 to 40 minutes
Summary and conclusion: 5 minutes

Activity

▶ Begin by explaining to the group that issues of grief and loss are often ignored or denied within all levels of an organisation, not just by the management (as is indeed the case in wider society). This exercise is designed to explore why this is and what might be done about it.

▶ **Step 1** – Divide the main group into subgroups and distribute copies of **Worksheet 8: It's got nothing to do with us**. Ask them to see how many reasons they can think of to explain why these issues are not often taken seriously. Encourage the groups to jot down their ideas on the worksheet.

NB. You might like to 'pump prime' the exercise by giving one or two examples yourself. You will probably need to circulate around the groups to give encouragement if any seem to be stuck.

▶ **Step 2** – Plenary discussion based on the findings of each group, which will be put up on display as each group reports. Open a discussion about any issues not covered on these lists.

▶ **Step 3** – Get everyone back into small groups, ideally with a different membership from Step 1. Distribute the flip chart sheets with the various reasons identified – one sheet per group, distributed at random. Each group should then be asked to debate each reason, evaluating its respective strengths and weaknesses and coming up with a reasoned response.

▶ **Step 4** – Reconvene the main group for a plenary discussion session based on the feedback from each group. Conclude by identifying specific issues which the group feels need to be addressed by your organisation and agree how these should be progressed.

▶ Use the last few minutes to summarise the main learning points to have emerged (or ask the group to do so).

Worksheet 8: It's got nothing to do with us

Loss and grief issues are often not taken seriously in organisations. What possible reasons for this can you identify?

Exercise 14: The conspiracy of silence

Aim

This exercise is an alternative to Exercise 13 and therefore has the same aim, namely: to explore reasons why organisations often do not take issues of grief and loss seriously in the workplace.

Materials

Flip chart paper and marker pens
Worksheet 9: The conspiracy of silence (1)
Worksheet 10: The conspiracy of silence (2)

Timing

This activity is likely to take about an hour, broken down roughly as follows:

Introduction: 5 minutes
Work in pairs: (Step 1) 5 to 10 minutes
Feedback and discussion: (Step 2) 20 minutes
Work with main group: (Step 3) 5 minutes
Work with main group: (Step 4) 20 minutes
Summary and conclusion: 5 minutes

Activity

▶ Begin by explaining to the group that the aim of this exercise is to explore why it is so often the case that organisations do not take issues of loss and grief seriously or may even disregard them altogether. Explain also that it will involve looking at 'the conspiracy of silence' – a term that refers to the tendency for such issues to be swept under the carpet and ignored.

▶ **Step 1** – Divide the main group into pairs and ask them, using **Worksheet 9: The conspiracy of silence (1)**, to note down as many euphemisms as they can for issues relating to death and dying ('passed on', 'kicked the bucket', 'went to meet their maker' and so on). Point out that this can be a fun exercise, but that they should draw a line at being offensive. You may need to circulate to support some of the less imaginative pairs.

▶ **Step 2** – After five or ten minutes, reconvene the main group. Ask them to call out (one at a time) their list of euphemisms and record these on the flip chart or board. Once you have the complete list, invite them to comment on the significance of having so many euphemisms for death and dying: what does this tell us about society's attitude to death and dying? Use this as a basis of a discussion to explore 'the conspiracy of silence'. You may also want to broaden this out to discuss losses other than death-related ones and ask whether society has a similar tendency to play down the role of loss and grief in people's lives.

▶ **Step 3 –** Next you should invite the whole group to work together to identify ways in which words relating to death and dying are commonly used in a 'sanitised' way – that is, with a meaning unconnected with their original. Examples include, 'dead tired', 'dying for a break'. Record these on the flip chart or board. There is no need to labour the point by spending too much time making a list of these – just enough to make the point that it is not the actual words we are afraid to use, but rather the whole topic of loss that has become something of a 'taboo' subject.

▶ **Step 4 –** Invite the group to suggest ways in which this taboo could possibly be broken within their organisation(s). List these on the flip chart or board and encourage the participants to make notes for future reference on **Worksheet 10: The conspiracy of silence (2)**.

▶ Use the last few minutes to summarise the main learning points to have emerged (or ask the group to do so).

Worksheet 9: The conspiracy of silence (1)

What euphemisms do we use to refer to death and dying? That is, what words or phrases do we use to avoid saying death-related words – for example, 'passed away' or 'kicked the bucket'?

Worksheet 10: The conspiracy of silence (2)

What steps can individuals and organisations take to break down the 'conspiracy of silence' and make it acceptable to talk openly about loss and grief?

Exercise 15: Men are from Mars...

Aim

To explore ways in which men and women might deal with issues of grief and loss in different ways and to consider the implications for such differences in terms of how we seek to support them.

Materials

Flip chart paper and marker pens
Worksheet 11: Men are from Mars...

Timing

This activity is likely to take about two hours, divided roughly as follows:

Introduction: 5 minutes
Groupwork: (Steps 1 and 2) 35 minutes
Feedback and discussion: (Step 3) 15 minutes
Presentation: (Step 4) 30 minutes
Feedback and discussion: (Step 5) 20 to 30 minutes
Summary and conclusion: (Step 6) 5 to 15 minutes

Activity

▶ We suggest that discussion starts around some storylines from some of the soaps on TV. You may or may not be a fan of EastEnders, Coronation Street, Hollyoaks, Neighbours and so on, but it would be helpful to have some recent story lines as memory joggers to start the group off.

▶ Explain to the group that it is often said that women and men differ in the ways in which they handle issues of grief and loss. Point out that there is research evidence to suggest that there is some truth in this, although it is not as simple or stereotyped as some people would have us believe.

▶ **Step 1** – Invite the participants to move into small groups and think of a story line from a current 'soap opera' on television which involves a major death or loss. How did the women react? How did the men react? Circulate among the groups to prompt any who seem to be stuck. If they struggle with soap operas, invite them to broaden it out to include films and TV dramas in general.

▶ **Step 2** – Staying in the same groups, invite them to compare the various reactions of the women and the men in the 'soaps' with 'real life' situations. How far is it true that women and men differ in how they react? Circulate among the groups to prompt any who seem to be stuck.

▶ **Step 3** – Next, reconvene the main group for a plenary discussion to list the main points identified by the groups. Note the agreements and disagreements and remind them that there are no definitive right or wrong answers.

▶ **Step 4** – Now you should make a brief presentation in which the following points need to be stressed:

 ▶ There are no right or wrong answers in this area – everyone has their own way of coping.

 ▶ It is probably true to say that many women find it easier than many men to handle the emotions associated with grief, and that a male way of coping can often be characterised by doing things which might enable them to process painful issues. But this does not mean that men do not have strong feelings.

 ▶ The Dual Process Model explained in Part One is a helpful way of understanding how both women and men handle issues of grief and loss. The loss orientation inevitably focuses on the emotional side of things, with the tears and the pain of the loss being uppermost; the restoration orientation focuses on everything to do with getting on with the rest of your life and the things which have to be done. Both women and men will spend significant amounts of time in each of these orientations, but how they do this will vary from individual to individual. It follows that unless there are serious problems, each person will do his or her best to get it right, and that other people should not get into the business of judging how others deal with it or make a judgement that somehow they are not 'doing it right'.

 ▶ Different work settings may highlight these issues in different ways. For example, a predominantly male organisation may well have a different culture in this respect than one which is mainly female. This may result in 'messages' being given by the majority about how the organisation expects its members to behave when under stress.

▶ **Step 5** – Reconvene the main group for a plenary discussion on the topic:

 ▶ How does all of this relate to your organisation?

 ▶ What implications does it have for how we try and support men and women who are grieving?

▶ If the participants are from the same organisation, then there should be interesting patterns that are likely to say something about the organisation's culture. If, however, the participants represent a number of different organisations, then this should present a useful opportunity to compare and contrast organisational cultures and how they relate to the complex and sensitive issues of loss and grief.

▶ Conclude this part of the exercise by summarising the main points from the discussion.

▶ **Step 6** – Ask the group to reflect on the session and, using **Worksheet 11: Men are from Mars…**, note down the single most important learning point that they will take away from this exercise. Allow a few minutes for this and then go round the group and ask each member to read out what has been, for him or her personally, the most important lesson to have been learned in this session. This should take a further three to ten minutes maximum, depending on the size of the group.

Worksheet 11: Men are from Mars...

This session has invited you to explore ways in which men and women might deal with issues of grief and loss in different ways. Please make a note – in one sentence if possible – of what has been the most important thing for you in this session, something of importance which you have learned.

You will be invited to read this out to the rest of the group to bring this session to a close. (You may also wish to use this sheet to make a brief note of what other participants have learned from the session.)

Exercise 16: Leaving was hard... but coming back was even worse

Aim

To explore issues around the challenges of returning to work after a time of bereavement or serious loss.

Materials

Flip chart and marker pens

Case study: Leaving was hard... but coming back was even worse – enough for one for each member of the group

Slide 8: Staff care (optional)

Slide 9: Returning to work – personal anxieties (optional)

Slide 10: Returning to work – Managers' and colleagues' anxieties (optional)

Handout 6: Returning to work

Worksheet 12: Leaving was hard... but coming back was even worse

Timing

This exercise is likely to take about two and a quarter hours, broken down roughly as follows:

Introduction: 5 minutes

Groupwork: (Step 1) 40 minutes

Feedback and discussion: (Step 2) 20 minutes

Groupwork: (Step 3) 30 minutes

Feedback and discussion: (Step 4) 30 minutes

Summary and conclusion: (Step 5) 15 minutes

Activity

▶ Explain that the purpose of this session is to explore some of the issues involved for people who have experienced serious loss when they seek to return to work. A case study has been provided to help people explore the issues in a hypothetical way through the case study scenario, and then to relate their 'findings' to their own workplace setting.

▶ **Step 1** – Divide the group into smaller groups of three or four per group, and hand them **Case study: Leaving was hard... but coming back was even worse**. Ask them to read it through, and then to respond to the issues outlined at the end of the case study. Circulate around the groups in case any appear to be stuck.

▶ **Step 2** – Reconvene the main group for a plenary feedback and discussion session. Ask participants to feedback verbally to the whole group – make a note on the flip chart of the main points being made. These could include:

  ▶ the impact of the sudden death upon Ishfaq of the loss of his wife and child

  ▶ the importance of cultural and religious observances – these will vary, of course

  ▶ the loss of creative drive due to the bereavement

  ▶ the difficulty of moving into a future orientation when he was not ready

  ▶ organisational denial of Ishfaq's needs

  ▶ unsupportive colleagues – the problems of competitive environments

  ▶ an apparent 'macho' male environment with assumptions about how everyone should cope

  ▶ management harassment, bullying and racism

  ▶ no strategy for a planned, gradual return to work.

▶ **Step 3** – Towards a model of best practice. Divide the main group into subgroups of three to four. Explain to them that their task is to draw up some guide lines for best practice in how to support people in making the difficult transition back into the workplace. Ask each group to record their key points on the flip chart.

▶ **Step 4** – Reconvene the main group for a plenary feedback and discussion session. Ask a representative from each group to present a brief report, displaying their flip chart sheets on the wall. Use the remaining time as an opportunity for a wide-ranging discussion of the main learning points.

▶ **Step 5** – Summary. The next step is to develop a summary. This should be based on **Handout 6: Returning to work**. Please feel free to adapt this to meet your needs more accurately. You may of course reproduce this handout in its present form.

NB. We also recommend that you read Chapter 8 of Neil Thompson's book *Stress Matters*, on which much of this summary has been based.

Worksheet 12: Leaving was hard... but coming back was even worse

1. Discuss what you believe to be the key issues in this scenario – identify the factors that caused Ishfaq's creativity to be diminished.

2. In what ways could his company have treated him differently?

Case study: Leaving was hard... but coming back was even worse

Ishfaq (aged 32) enjoyed his job in a busy advertising department of a large multinational company dealing in fashion design. He had a particular flair for eye-catching slogans and slightly 'wacky' photo shoot opportunities, which often gave him the edge over other team members when it came to major promotional developments. The executive board had tended to choose Ishfaq's designs over the past eight years, and sales records had more than justified their faith in his designs. The company was thriving.

One evening in winter Ishfaq was working late when he had an urgent telephone call from the local hospital. His wife, who was seven months pregnant with their first child, had been knocked down by the car on her way home. The driver had been found to have been over the alcohol limit. Ishfaq rushed to the hospital but was greeted with the news upon arrival that his wife had died ten minutes ago. He was distraught.

In accordance with company policy Ishfaq was granted two weeks' compassionate leave, which he subsequently augmented with two further weeks' annual leave, although this request was granted somewhat begrudgingly by his manager who reminded him of the important new contract they had won, and that they were expecting Ishfaq to deliver the winning design once more. The manager hinted that he expected Ishfaq to be working on his designs at home in readiness to present preliminary drawings to the executive team on his second day back at work.

The month away from work proved traumatic for him. His extended family expected him to arrange not only the funeral, but a variety of other events which marked the family's mourning for his wife. He found this very exhausting and realised that his previous overworking had left him with little energy to cope with this crisis in his life. He had received a couple of cards from colleagues at work, but they clearly had little understanding of his cultural background or the religious and family demands being made of him. He also realised that his success had caused resentment among several colleagues who lacked his flair and imagination.

The weekend before his scheduled return to work, Ishfaq took up his laptop and tried for the first time in a month to develop ideas for new designs. After several hours he gave up, defeated and dejected: the ideas simply would not flow.

He dragged himself to work on the Monday morning and was present in time for the usual start of week team meeting. The manager briefly welcomed him back and proceeded to outline the strategy for the next day's presentation. He then invited Ishfaq to present his designs for discussion. Ishfaq explained that, due to his bereavement, he had not been able to achieve anything – he would keep on trying, but for once he had hoped that other colleagues would be able to deliver the goods. He was met with a stony silence. The manager then swept out of the office, telling Ishfaq he had 24 hours to deliver his designs or else.

For the rest of the day Ishfaq did what he could, but sensed that colleagues were holding back, waiting him for him to fail, rather than supporting and helping him. He worked until late, but he knew that his usual creative flair was missing.

At the design meeting next day he presented his ideas which he knew would not be accepted. To his amazement two other colleagues followed his presentation with their own ideas, one of which received the executive's reluctant approval as 'the best that could be hoped for in these regrettable circumstances'. Feeling increasingly uncomfortable, Ishfaq left work early, claiming he was feeling unwell. The following day his letter of resignation was found on the chief executive's desk.

Exercise 17: Oh my God!

Aim

To help people explore issues of religion and spirituality and their relationship to grief and loss.

Materials

Flip chart and marker pens
Handout 7: Oh my God!

Timing

This activity is likely to take between 60 and 90 minutes, roughly divided as follows:

Introduction: (Step 1)10 to 15 minutes
Groupwork: (Step 2) 10 to 15 minutes
Discussion and feedback: (Step 3) 40 to 55 minutes
Summary and conclusion: (Step 4) 5 minutes

Activity

▶ An introductory handout has been prepared for this session. You may wish to introduce it yourself, or alternatively suggest that for the first ten minutes people take time to read it through carefully once or twice to help set the scene for this session. It is worth remembering that, as the trainer, you are unlikely to know where your group members are 'coming from' as far as issues of religion and spirituality are concerned. Your own perspective on these issues may not be known to the group. It is important, therefore, to set the tone well for this session so that everyone's point of view is listened to respectfully.

▶ **Step 1** – Distribute copies of **Handout 7: Oh my God!** to each member of the group, with a brief scene-setting statement from yourself to explain that the handout sets the context for the session.

▶ **Step 2** – Having given people time to read the handout, ask them to get into groups of two or three and spend about ten minutes in discussion, with each member beginning with the statement:

'I find it difficult to talk to other people about religion because...'

▶ **Step 3** – Invite some plenary feedback on these discussions, which will give you a 'feel' for how easily or otherwise people are engaging with this subject. Follow this with further plenary discussion by asking the group about the following questions:

1. What did they make of the presence of so many religious leaders at the scene of Ground Zero after September 11th?

2. What role do they think religious leaders should play at people's funerals?

3. Do they think religious leaders have a role to play with people who have experienced serious loss?

4. Do they think their organisation ought to have a chaplain? If so, what would that role involve?

5. Do they think that a divine being is to be held responsible in any way for human suffering?

▶ **Step 4** – The discussion in Step 3 will inevitably be a wide-ranging discussion in which a range of views is likely to be expressed. It will probably not have a neat and tidy conclusion – it is more likely that you will need simply to draw the discussion to a close by reminding people of the importance of these issues, and the need to respect the wide variety of views held by many people in the workplace.

Part Three: Conclusion

Concluding comments

You will perhaps have realised already that this training manual is pitched at a basic and introductory level. So much more could have been included on the subject of loss and grief in the workplace, given the enormity of the topic and the long-standing tendency for it to be neglected. However, we have had to be realistic in terms of how much ground we can cover in one manual. We are aware that the issues covered are both complex and sensitive, and we would certainly not want to encourage anyone to run before they can walk.

Our intention has not been to produce 'the last word' – far from it. From our point of view, if this manual enables you to move from feeling uncertain and hesitant about how to plan and run training sessions in this difficult area, to a point where you are running such events successfully and perhaps on a regular basis, we will feel that this manual has been a success – even more so if you then move on to explore these issues in greater depth using other resource materials, perhaps beginning with the suggestions in this section.

Every working day across the various sectors of industry, business and commerce, public service and the armed forces, there are people who are feeling the adverse effects of a major loss in their lives, whether that be a death-related loss or one associated with other major transitions in our lives, such as a divorce or relationship breakdown, or a loss of our dreams or aspirations – as we have seen in this manual, losses are many and varied. To neglect the significance of loss in the workplace is to leave a major part of organisational life – and a potentially major source of problems and difficulties – untouched. The price an organisation can pay for failing to take account of loss and grief can be very high indeed. Continuing to neglect such issues is clearly a mistake, and we hope that this manual can play a part in making sure that such mistakes become far less common than is currently the case.

There is much talk these days about the importance of 'emotional intelligence', which involves the ability both to read other people's emotional responses and be 'tuned in' to what our own emotions are telling us in particular situations. If we are to be serious about the value of emotional intelligence as an important factor in successful organisations, then clearly loss, as a source of intense emotion, is not something that we can afford to ignore.

This manual has provided an overview of many of the important issues and concepts that we need to grasp if we are to understand loss and grief sufficiently to be able to tackle these matters in a workplace setting. It has also presented a number of exercises that can be used to mount training courses, either as they are or in an adapted form if you feel confident enough to develop materials in this way. We hope that the materials we have provided may also spur you to think of further training activities based on your own particular organisation or work setting.

In this final section, we provide suggestions for further reading and details of relevant organisations and websites. These are intended to act as a gateway to further study and learning. What we have provided here is very much a starting point, rather than a comprehensive or exhaustive account, and so we do hope that you will take the opportunity to develop your understanding as fully as you can. The more you understand these difficult issues, the better equipped you will be to deal with them – in a training context or indeed in life more broadly.

In our view, it is the starting that is the hardest in this field, especially as it is a topic that is so often neglected or disregarded altogether. Once you have gained confidence, we feel that the manual will have proved a success. We would therefore welcome and appreciate any feedback you would like to give about this manual from your experience of using it. We wish you well in using it and in tackling the major challenges of dealing with loss and grief in the workplace.

Guide to further learning

Recommended reading

Here are a few suggestions for further reading to help you develop your understanding of these issues. There is a vast literature available: these books, we believe, will provide an excellent starting place for further reading and study. For full details, please see the References section on the next page.

Aries, P. (1981) *The Hour of Our Death.*
A classic text that has proven very influential in shaping our thinking.

Attig, T. (2000) *The Heart of Grief: Death and the Search for Lasting Love*
Attig, T. (2010) *How We Grieve: Relearning the World*
Two books from a very well-respected author. Both have significant insights to offer.

Corr, C. M., Corr, D. M. and Doka, K. J. (2018) *Death and Dying, Life and Living.*
This is a very thorough and well-written American textbook. It provides a very comprehensive overview.

Doka, K. J. and Martin, T. L. (2010) *Grieving Beyond Gender: Understanding the Ways Men and Women Mourn.*
This book addresses gender issues in relation to loss and grief.

Morgan, J. and Laungani, P. (2002) *Death and Bereavement Around the World: Major Religious Traditions.*
A really valuable introduction to major religions and their attitudes towards death and dying.

Thompson, N. (2012) *Grief and its Challenges*
A clear and helpful guide to making sense of grief.

Thompson, N. and Cox, G. R. (eds) (2018) *Handbook of the Sociology of Death, Grief, and Bereavement.*
A book with a sociological emphasis that provides an important counterbalance to the strong psychological bias in the literature relating to death, dying and bereavement.

Thompson, N. (2009) *Loss, Grief and Trauma in the Workplace.*
Essential reading for anyone needing to understand these issues in a workplace environment.

References

Aries, P. (1981) *The Hour of Our Death*, Oxford, Oxford University Press.

Attig , T. (2000) *The Heart of Grief*, Oxford and New York, Oxford University Press.

Attig, T. (2010) *How We Grieve: Re-learning the World*, 2nd edn, Oxford, Oxford University Press.

Bowlby, J. (1991) *Loss: Sadness and Depression, Attachment and Loss 3*, Harmondsworth, Penguin.

Corr, C. M., Corr, D. M. and Doka, K. J. (2018) *Death and Dying, Life and Living*, 9th edn. Boston, MA, Cengage Learning.

Doka, K. J. (ed.} (1989) *Disenfranchised Grief: Recognizing Hidden Sorrow*, Lexington, MA, Lexington Books (now also in 3rd edn, 2001).

Doka, K. J. and Martin, T. L. (2010) *Grieving Beyond Gender: Understanding the Ways Men and Women Mourn*, 2nd edn, New York, Routledge.

Fitzgerald, H. (1999) *Grief at Work – A Manual of Policies and Practices*, Washington, DC, American Hospice Foundation.

Klass, D., Silverman P. R. and Nickman, S. L. (eds) (1996) *Continuing Bonds, New Understandings of Grief*, London, Taylor and Francis.

Kubler-Ross, E. (1969) *On Death and Dying*, New York, Macmillan.

Morgan, J. and Laungani, P. (2002) *Death and Bereavement Around the World: Major Religious Traditions*, Amityvillle, NY, Baywood.

Moss, B. R. (2002) *'Spirituality: A Personal Perspective'*, in Thompson (2002).

Moss, B. R. (2005) *Religion and Spirituality*, Lyme Regis, Russell House Publishing. Neimeyer, R. A. and Anderson, A. (2002) 'Meaning Reconstruction Theory', in Thompson (2002).

Parkes, C. M. (2010) *Bereavement*, 4th edn, London and New York, Routledge.

Schneider, J. (2012) *Finding My Way: From Trauma to Transformation*, Traverse City, MI, Seasons Press.

Stroebe, M. and Schut, H. (1999) *'The Dual Process Model of Coping with Bereavement: Rationale and Description'*, Death Studies 23(3).

Thompson, N. (ed.) (2002) *Loss and Grief: A Guide for Human Services Practitioners*, Basingstoke, Palgrave Macmillan.

Thompson, N. (2009) *Loss, Grief and Trauma in the Workplace*, New York, Routledge.

Thompson, N. (2012) *Grief and its Challenges*, Basingstoke, Palgrave Macmillan.

Thompson, N. (2015) *Stress Matters*, an e-book published by Avenue Media Solutions.

Thompson, N. and Cox, G. R. (eds) (2018) *Handbook of the Sociology of Death, Grief, and Bereavement*, New York, Routledge.

Walter, T. (1999) *On Bereavement: The Culture of Grief*, Buckingham, Open University Press.

Worden, W. (2009) *Grief Counseling and Grief Therapy: A Handbook for the Mental Health Practitioner*, 4th edn, New York, NY, Springer Publishing Company.

Please note that, while every effort has been made to check the accuracy of the information listed below, changes do often occur. It may also be the case that some of the organisations, whose national details we provide, may also have local branches with details in your local directory. Up-to-date information is also always available through any reputable search engine on the internet.

Organisations

Asian Family Counselling Service

F1 Hampton Court
George Road
Birmingham, B15 1PU
https://asianfamilycounselling.org

or

F1 Unit 4
Triangle Centre
399 Uxbridge Road
Southall
London, UB1 3EJ

British Association of Counselling and Psychotherapy

BACP House, 15 St John's Business Park Lutterworth, LE17 4HB
01445 883300
www.bacp.co.uk

British Humanist Association (Help and advice with secular funerals and so on)

Humanists UK
39 Moreland St
London, EC1V 8BB
02073 243060
www.humanism.org.uk

Child Bereavement UK

www.childbereavement.org.uk

The Compassionate Friends UK

03451 203875 (Helpline)
www.tcf.org.uk

CRUSE Bereavement Care (Free confidential help to bereaved people)

PO B0x 800

Richmond, TW9 1RG

Helpline (England, Northern Ireland and Wales): 08088 091677

Cruse Scotland: 08456 002227

www.cruse.org.uk

Jewish Bereavement Counselling Service

The Maurice and Vivienne Wohal Campus

221 Golders Green Road

London, NW11 9DQ

02089 513881

Lesbian and Gay Bereavement Project

Friend

86 Caledonian Road

London, N1 9DN

02078 331675

https://peopleforstinfo.org.uk/marketplace/cat/vendor/1640

The Lullaby Trust (Infant death support)

11, Belgrave Road

London, SW1V 1RB

0808 802 6868 (Helpline) helpline@fsid.org.uk www.fsid .org.uk

RoadPeace

Unit F6 Shakespeare Business Centre

245a Coldharbour Lane

London SW9 8RR

02077 331603

Samaritans (For those experiencing despair, distress or suicidal feelings)

Free from any phone (UK and ROI)

116123

Stillbirth and Neonatal Death Society (SANDS)

Victoria Charity Centre

11 Belgrave Road

London, SW1V 1RB

www.sands.org.uk

Helpline 08081 643332

Sudden
www.suddendeath.org

Support after Murder and Manslaughter (SAMM)
L &DCTally Ho!
Pershore Road
Edgebaston
B5 7RN
01214 722912
www.samm.org.uk

Survivors of Bereavement by Suicide (SOBS)
National Office
Flamstead Centre
Albert St
Ilkeston
DE7 5GU
Helpline 03001 115065

Terrence Higgins Trust (Information and support about HIV and sexual health)
314-329 Grays Inn Rd
London, WC1X 8DP
02078 121600
www.tht.org.uk

Winston's Wish (Child bereavement charity)
01242 515157
www.winstonswish.org.uk

Internet resources

In addition to the internet resources listed in the Organisations section above, the following websites can be useful sources of relevant information:

www.growthhouse.org/

This is an award-winning portal to resources that cover a range of life-threatening illnesses and end-of-life care. The organisation aims to educate and raise the standards of care of people in such situations. In addition to providing information and advice about specific conditions, it also deals with broader issues, such as palliative care and dealing with grief. It has a bookstore and a professional forum.

www.doh.gov.uk/bereavement

Part of the Department of Health life events section, this site gives help on practical issues and emotional aspects of bereavement. It makes reference to resources in the separate parts of the UK.

www.uk-sobs.org.uk/about

The UK site of SOBS, a voluntary organisation that supports those who have been bereaved by the loss of a relative or friend who has committed suicide. It includes details of telephone contacts, residential events and conferences, and how to obtain a bereavement pack. It provides the telephone numbers of a wide range of organisations dealing with loss issues (03001 115065).

www.samaritans.org.uk

Here you will find the opportunity to learn about the history, vision and values of the Samaritans, as well as to receive or offer help. It gives access to relevant publications and reports and has links with other organisations such as Depression Alliance, Childline, Mind and Befrienders International (116123).

www.silentgrief.com

This site offers support to those who have experienced miscarriage or the loss of an older child. It has a 'chat board' and access to articles and resources.

www.humansolutions.org.uk

This is a site offering information and advice on 'people problems' in organisations. It has a section on loss and grief in the workplace.

www.adec.org

Association for Death Education and Counselling (ADEC). A dedicated educational site providing its members and general public with information, support and resources based on theoretical and quality research. It offers helpful information across the lifespan and relating to a very wide range of contexts in relation to death, dying and bereavement. It also offers useful links.

www.grief.org.au

Australian Centre for Grief and Bereavement. An organisation dedicated to developing and providing a range of specialist interventions and innovative education services, informed by evidence-based practice, for grieving people who are at risk of adverse outcomes. It also provides grief education and a range of consultancy services to develop and enhance the capacity of individuals, organisations and communities to deal effectively with loss. In addition, it provides information regarding grief and bereavement counselling training and supervision. It also provides advocacy and representation on grief and bereavement issues in order to inform policy development, raise community awareness and support universal access to mainstream grief and bereavement services.

www.genesis-resources. com

Genesis Bereavement Resources. This is a Canadian website dedicated to providing a whole range of services to those involved in this area. It provides monthly articles on bereavement, grief and loss with back issues easily available on the website. It sells books, videos and DVDs aimed at a wide audience from children to older people.

www.hospicefoundation.org

Hospice Foundation of America. This site is full of information for anyone to tap into. It provides a wide range of links on areas related to this topic. It offers information in a variety of media – audio, visual and written – that is easily accessible from the website. It also offers an annual Bereavement Teleconference led by leading figures in the field of bereavement studies. A monthly e-newsletter includes individual narratives where people can share their experiences of the grief process. In addition, it provides volunteer workers who work in the community.

www.iwgddb.org

The International Work Group on Death, Dying and Bereavement. Contains details of publications produced by members of this important group.

www.workplacetraumacenter.com

The Workplace Trauma Center. A site that offers training and a response service worldwide. It provides information for the layperson on dealing with the aftermath of workplace violence and trauma. It specialises in workplace violence intervention, violence management, training services and robbery survival skills.

Appendix:
The handouts

Handout 1

Approach 1: The Dual Process Model

A very good starting place for our understanding of how people grieve is a relatively new 'dance' that has been called the 'Dual Process Model'. Like so many other people working in this field, its authors (Margaret Stroebe and Henk Schut) noticed that many people who experience profound loss have a remarkable ability to do two things at once. We may best illustrate this with an example.

Picture a woman who has been recently bereaved. She is at home by herself, in emotional turmoil. She is distressed, disorientated, pottering aimlessly about the house. Suddenly the doorbell rings. Drying her eyes, adjusting her hair and face, she opens the door, and deals with having to sign for a package. Back indoors, she gets on with some household chores – gets upset – and then the phone rings. Putting on a 'brave face' she takes the call, and deals with it in a calm and efficient way.

And so, her day and her week and her months go by. At times she is distraught, on other occasions she is 'more like her normal self' and can get on with things in a practical way. She has good days and bad days.

She is not alone in this, for it is a common experience for many people who are grieving. Stroebe and Schut called this the Dual Process Model because they suggest that all grieving people deal with two quite different processes at one and the same time. The first involves all the horrible feelings which have been stirred up by the loss. At every turn, the person is faced with the implications of their loss – it is LOSS in capital letters and there is no getting away from it. The second is what is often called 'getting on with the rest of your life', or 'restoration', as Stroebe and Schut describe it. It involves all the 101 things that still need to be done, but also moves into the different ways of living which slowly become possible as a new future is faced.

The important thing about this way of understanding is that these two aspects of living – or 'orientations' as Stroebe and Schut call them – go along side by side, and grieving people move from one to the other and back again on a regular basis. In the early days they are likely to be much more in the loss aspect, with occasional moments in the restoration aspect. But, as time goes by, the balance shifts, and at some point a person will find that far more time is being spent with a future focus as they get on with their lives. But – and it is a big but – there will always be moments, often unguarded, when they find themselves back in the loss aspect – feeling the loss. Key dates like birthdays will often trigger these feelings, and it may take many years before the sharpness diminishes.

In this way of looking at the grief and loss, we should expect there to be times and occasions when the grieving person is upset and 'down in the dumps' – it is natural, and perhaps should even be welcomed as a reminder of the ways in which life was enhanced and enriched by the person who has now died.

Handout 2

Approach 2: The idea of stages

Without doubt, this approach is the one most likely to be quoted by a wide range of people, including many professionals, when asked about how people deal with grief and loss. It owes its origin to Elizabeth Kùbler-Ross who worked as a psychiatrist for many years with dying and bereaved people, but similar approaches have been suggested by other equally eminent practitioners, such as John Bowlby and Colin Murray Parkes.

This approach was based on observations of many dying and bereaved people, where some common themes were noted. These included:

▶ **DENIAL:** an immediate reaction to the news of someone's death is the refusal to believe it is true – it can't have happened.

▶ **NUMBNESS:** part of the denial – people can draw into themselves with the shock of bad news – feelings can be too painful, so we 'shut down' and refuse to allow ourselves to hurt.

▶ **ANGER:** feelings begin to tumble out of us, without any clear focus or direction – we hurt more than we can say, and we lash out with our tongues at anyone and everyone.

▶ **DEPRESSION:** the anger gets turned in upon ourselves – we feel we cannot cope and we may even feel suicidal – life feels not worth living without our loved one.

▶ **ACCEPTANCE:** we 'come to terms' with our loss, and begin to rebuild our lives and face a new future.

This is a very basic description of the stages through which a grieving person may pass, and more recently this basic model has been expanded to make it more comprehensive and detailed, and also refined to make it feel less mechanistic.

Many of the 'stages' ring bells with a lot of people who can identify with the feelings. Some people find it a comfort that one stage seems to lead to another and that it is a way of reassuring people that there is a 'light at the end of the tunnel'.

It needs to be said, however, that a growing consensus of contemporary writers has led to a movement away from even a sophisticated 'stages model', because they feel that it does not do justice to the complexity and variety of people's reactions to grief and loss and runs the risk of being seen as a prescriptive model.

Handout 3

Approach 3: The tasks of grief

Another way of helping us understand what grief is all about was offered by William Worden, who moved away from the idea of stages or processes. He suggested that a helpful way to understand what grief is all about is to identify a number of tasks which a grieving person would need successfully to complete in order to move into the future.

The word 'tasks' may be a little off-putting at first – it is not like having a list of jobs to do, like going shopping, paying the rent, or doing your washing. Worden has much more psychological tasks in mind, which is hardly surprising as he was deeply involved in grief counselling and issues in people's mental health. He identified four main areas where, if you like, work has to be done if grief is to be successfully tackled.

▶ **Task One:** To accept the reality of the loss.

▶ **Task Two:** To work through the pain of grief.

▶ **Task Three:** To adjust to a world without the deceased (externally, internally and spiritually).

▶ **Task Four:** To move on emotionally.

It is important to recognise that these are not strictly sequential: it is not a case that you cannot tackle Task Three until Tasks One and Two have been thoroughly accomplished – far from it. For many people, it takes a long, long time before Task One is achieved and maybe for some it is never finally complete. Some people are caught up into Task Two immediately; others find that it takes a long time before they really let the pain of the event find full expression.

So, these are almost parallel tasks, except that Task Four makes it clear that, until some measure of 'letting go' has been achieved, it will be difficult to get on with life. However, Worden also recognises this is more of adaptation, and that 'eventually moving on' may also involve keeping an enduring connection or continuing bond with the deceased. There are some people for whom this is particularly difficult, who may need skilled help to complete this particular task.

For many people, the usefulness of this approach is that it highlights the importance of our being involved, and seeking to take charge, to some extent at least, of what is happening to us. Although there will be times when we sit back and let things swamp us and overcome us, we will need to find the energy to tackle these tasks, knowing that there is a different future ahead over which we have some control.

Handout 4

Approach 4: Finding new meanings

A common strand running through a lot of people's experience of grief is the loss of any meaning and purpose as a result of their great loss. They had vested so much in this particular relationship that its destruction shattered that sense of meaning for them.

That this is a key theme is beyond doubt, not least because without some sense of meaning and purpose most of us find it difficult to get on with our lives. This is not to deny some of the great strands of postmodernism which are woven into contemporary society, and which state that it is now increasingly difficult, if not impossible, to believe any more in grand overarching themes which can give meaning and purpose to our lives. That is something which you may wish to debate. At an individual level, however, most of us find something of this sense of meaning and purpose through particular relationships, and, when these cease, we find ourselves struggling to find a way forward without them.

This links both the fourth task identified by Worden (see Handout 3), and also with another set of approaches which focus on this issue of meaning. Some of the language of previous approaches had been that of 'working through' one's grief; of being able to 'let go' and 'move on' – all of which resonate to some extent with people's experience of grief and loss.

Some more recent approaches, however, encourage more of a narrative or 'story telling' approach which seeks not so much to leave things behind, as to reshape our understanding of where we are, and who we are, in the light of the loss we have experienced. Many bereaved people will readily talk of their loved one still being with them, many years after their physical death. For some, of course, this has a specific spiritual dimension because of a particular religious faith. But others, without this spirituality, will still talk of their lives being influenced by the memory of their loved one; of the 'gap still being very much there' in their lives, which nothing can fill.

Writers who have been exploring this aspect of grieving are now talking about 'story telling' in the sense of reshaping the sense of meaning and purpose after a significant loss – 'meaning reconstruction', for example, is a phrase used by Robert Neimeyer and his colleagues in the United States and Tony Walter in the UK that emphasises the importance of retelling the story of the loved one so that it has contemporary significance.

There is something in the 'reshaping of the biography of the deceased' which releases it from the past and makes it part of our present. 'Getting over a loss', from this perspective, is less a product of counselling or treatment, and a much more creative, albeit painful, reshaping of our individual world in the aftermath of the loss.

Handout 5

My boss really cares

▶ Are there guidelines for compassionate leave?

▶ What is an employee who has been bereaved entitled to expect?

▶ Are there arrangements for an employee to be able to take unpaid leave without losing their basic rights?

▶ Does the organisation allow flexi-working to help people experiencing grief and loss return to their employment?

▶ Health and safety: does the organisation recognise that people experiencing the stress of loss and grief may have reduced capacity to operate machinery and equipment safely?

▶ If there are major critical incidents in your organisation, how would employees be cared for effectively to help avoid the disabling symptoms of post-traumatic stress?

▶ Does your organisation have a confidential counselling service or 'employee assistance programme'?

Handout 6

Returning to work

On returning to work after a period of compassionate leave following the stress of a major loss, a person may feel anxious about:

- ▶ How workmates, colleagues and managers will react

- ▶ The extent to which 'things have moved on' without me – 'Am I still needed and valued?'

- ▶ Will I be able to cope at my job?

- ▶ Will I make a fool of myself and burst into tears when people ask how I am?

- ▶ Will I be able to get back to speed quickly enough? Or ever?

These anxieties are what Thompson (2015) calls 'Dealing with the Aftermath' of a major stressful event, and are part of what he calls 'the sometimes difficult transition back into 'normal' working life'.

These anxieties are mirrored by those experienced by colleagues and managers who may well feel anxious about the following:

- ▶ Have they come back to work too soon?

- ▶ What can I say to them?

- ▶ Should I mention their loss and ask how they are?

- ▶ Is it best just to ignore them and get on with it?

- ▶ Will they be able to cope with the job?

- ▶ Will we have to carry them?

- ▶ If so, for how long?

These are also part of 'Dealing with the Aftermath', and it is easy to see how two matching sets of anxieties can conspire to make the return to work doubly problematic.

There are clearly major responsibilities for management to ensure that a proper assessment is made about a person's fitness to return to work, once they have received medical clearance of course. An initial interview needs to be held as soon as the person is medically cleared to return to work following a period of extended absence, to clarify and talk through some of the issues which have caused anxiety on both sides.

A major issue will be whether or not the person requires some degree of workload relief to enable them to get back into the swing of things at work. This is admittedly difficult to calculate in order to strike a balance between the de-skilling effect of having too little to do, and the contrasting overload of work before a person's resilience has fully returned.

Finally

Returning to work after a period of loss-related absence can be a difficult process for all concerned – the member of staff involved, his or her colleagues and the line manager. Each has a part to play in contributing to the success or otherwise of the process of reintegration.

Handout 7

Oh my God!

Many people, whether or not they have a religious allegiance, instinctively exclaim the title of this exercise when faced with bad news. For some it is a powerful exclamation and nothing more; for others, it is an expression of some sort of faith in a higher being; and for others it is literally a prayer for help to a divine being in whom they have placed their trust.

This exercise is designed to help people explore some of the issues around religion and spirituality, not least because major traumas like loss and bereavement can often stop people in their tracks and cause them to ask questions about the meaning of their lives which otherwise might have gone unasked.

In contemporary multicultural societies, there are still many people who belong to faith communities. Christianity, Islam and Judaism command major followings, but there are many other religions which people find attractive and compelling. One common feature of all religions is the sense of meaning which they can give to people's lives, and also the meaning which they can often give to people's death and dying. What people believe happens to them when they die is one of the seminal questions we all have to face, and the answers we give will tell people a lot about how we feel we should live our lives.

The question of meaning is also caught up with the issue of spirituality, which is notoriously difficult to define. For some people, spirituality is inextricably bound up with their religion and how they practise it. For many others, however, it is a far more diffuse concept, and one that is encapsulated in the broad issue of what gives people meaning and purpose in their lives.

At times of serious loss, however, people's faith can be sorely tested, and the sense of meaning and purpose which previously underpinned their lives can be dislocated, if not shattered. It is therefore important to have some understanding of this dimension of human experience, and for us to be able to appreciate other people's experience and perspectives.